NOT JUST ANOTHER SCIENCE FAIR

A HANDBOOK AND MORE FOR SCIENCE FAIR ORGANIZERS

LAURA VAZQUEZ

▼

DAVID M. FRANCE
UNIVERSITY OF ILLINOIS AT CHICAGO

▼

KIM M. PERKINS

▼

GoodYearBooks

An Imprint of ScottForesman
A Division of HarperCollins*Publishers*

NOT JUST ANOTHER
SCIENCE
FAIR

Dedication: *This book is dedicated to the students,*

those who have grown with us,

and those who will grow through its use.

GoodYearBooks are available
for most basic curriculum subjects
plus many enrichment areas.
For more GoodYearBooks,
contact your local bookseller
or educational dealer.
For a complete catalog with
information about other
GoodYearBooks, please write:

GoodYearBooks

ScottForesman
1900 East Lake Avenue
Glenview, IL 60025

Book design and cover illustration by Patricia Lenihan-Barbee.

IBM is a registered trademark of International Business Machines, Inc.
Apple and Macintosh are registered trademarks of Apple Computer, Inc.
Hewlett-Packard LaserJet III is a product of Hewlett-Packard Company.
WordPerfect 5.1™ is a trademark of WordPerfect Corporation.

2 3 4 5 6 7 8 9 - MP - 02 01 00 99 98 97 96 95 94

0-673-36132-2

Scientists

have odious manners,

except when

you prop up

their theory;

then you can borrow

money of them.

Mark Twain, *Essays*

About the authors: The backgrounds of the authors of this book reflect the same valuable blend that is important to a successful Science Fair Steering Committee: science, community, and education. David France is a researcher, author, and university professor of engineering. His background brings both expertise in science and familiarity with science education, through the college level, to the process. Laura Vazquez is involved with education and is a representative of a local school-community support group. Her experience in science, education, and community leadership provides a strong blend of service to the fair efforts. Kim Perkins contributes the perspective of an educator to the fair, given his background as an elementary- and middle-school principal. All three are parents as well.

A Science Fair Steering Committee with the advantageous overlap of backgrounds—community leaders, scientists, educators, and parents—can greatly enhance the strength and potential success of any fair, as the authors have found in developing the community-based fair and in preparing this book. The diversity of such a pool of talent also balances the workload associated with an undertaking of this type and enhances the quality of the event.

Acknowledgments: The material presented in this book was developed over eight years in Elementary School District #44, Lombard, Illinois. We would like to express our appreciation for the help that was freely given during all of those development years when, at times, events became trying. We were fortunate to have received a start from the Friends of the Gifted and Talented of Downers Grove, formerly a chapter of the Illinois Council for the Gifted. We thank the members of this school support group for sharing their experiences with us and providing a framework from which to develop our science fair. The Lombard community support group, PALS (People Actively Lending Support), led in adapting this initial framework; there would have been no science fair without their diligence and effort.

Through the years of development, many individuals within District #44 dedicated substantial time and effort to the science fair. We gratefully acknowledge the important roles they played. A few individuals participated repeatedly, and we wish to acknowledge them individually. Special thanks to: Ms. Joanne Born, Ms. Sandra Matalis, Mr. Michael Pylypczak, and Ms. Dorothy Young for their special efforts during the early development years; and Mr. James Adams, Ms. Donna France, and Ms. Sandra Truax for their continued support every year.

WE HEAR alarming reports that our students are lagging behind other countries in science. To what extent these concerns are warranted is unclear. But as parents and teachers, we can help students in science; we do not have to be scientists to do it! *NOT JUST ANOTHER SCIENCE*

FAIR is designed to provide one set of resources in this effort. It is based on our own experiences during eight years of developing a successful science fair experience for students from kindergarten through eighth grade. In the following pages you will find a complete program for how to reproduce a similar fair in your community. *T*here are hundreds of books on science fairs, but most of them are only about how to do science-fair projects. This book is about *HOW TO ORGANIZE AN EXCITING COMMUNITY SCIENCE FAIR,* and it provides direction in applying the scientific method to student projects. *COMMUNITY IS A KEY WORD* for us since our science fair is much more than a traditional one-day event. It consists of four stimulating and motivating events aimed at teaching students and parents together about *DOING SCIENCE EXPERIMENTS*—not just demonstrations or surveys. We focus on producing memorable hands-on experiences in science, providing interaction with people engaged in science and engineering who are enthusiastic about their fields, and creating an exciting atmosphere that will not soon be forgotten. To do all of this, community support of the schools is essential. *T*his book contains *COMPLETE ORGANIZATIONAL MATERIALS* for the science fair events including lists of community and school personnel–their functions and responsibilities. In addition to an *ORGANIZATION CHART,* time lines of events, starting from the initial set-up of the Science Fair Steering Committee in the fall to the post-fair evaluation in the spring, provide detailed guidelines. The details of performing a science experiment in *NOT JUST ANOTHER SCIENCE FAIR* are accompanied by complete examples. All printed material used in the events of the fair are given in figures, tables, in the *APPENDICES,* and on the *ACCOMPANYING COMPUTER DISK.* We have included a complete *SCIENCE FAIR HANDBOOK* in reproducible form, to be given to parents and students to guide them through both a science experiment and the science fair itself. The disk files will facilitate tailoring these materials to your own fair. Also included on the disk is a computer program to be used the day of the science fair to make assigning project awards fast and fair. We wrote this program to eliminate the problem of the "hard" judge versus the "easy" judge; we are not aware of any other similar material. This point of *FAIRNESS IN JUDGING* is essential to the credibility of the fair—students deserve no less. *O*ur science fair is based on *OUR EXTENSIVE EXPERIENCE* with students, their parents, teachers, and community leaders. Because it has grown into a well-organized event, this fair is a pleasure to attend, fun to participate in, and fair in the judging of students' work. It is much more than just another science fair, and we present all of the details so yours will be equally successful. Whether you are starting a science fair for the first time or restructuring an existing fair, we are convinced that the following plans will provide you with the guidelines you need in creating worthwhile and *MEMORABLE EXPERIENCES IN SCIENCE* for students in your community.

CONTENTS

Chapter **3**

SCIENCE EXPERIMENTS: A HOW-TO GUIDE ♦ ♦ ♦ 58

FIGURES

ELECTRICAL FRUIT!!

NOT JUST ANOTHER SCIENCE FAIR

▼

EQUATING FUN AND SCIENCE

Who shall criticize the builders? Certainly not those who have stood idly by without lifting a stone.

E. T. Bell

■ *There is little argument that interest in science has declined in the U.S. in recent years. It is anticipated that our country will soon need 500,000 more scientists and engineers than our colleges and universities are producing. There is certainly cause for concern regarding the number of scientists and science educators we will have for the future. Projected shortages have led to increases in scholarship funds to encourage the teaching of science at all levels.*

But current instructional practice in science is also a cause for concern. For a variety of unfortunate reasons, elementary science courses are often taught with little or no hands-on experience. Students can be bored at the elementary level by science taught solely by discussion and memorization. From such an approach year after year, students can be systematically turned off to science. By the time they reach high school, many are disenchanted by the perceived complexity of chemistry or physics rather than intrigued by the questions these subjects ask about our world. The way in which science is presented at an early age can significantly influence a student's feeling toward what should be an interesting and exciting field. The shortage of scientists in the future and the extent of science literacy nationwide lay in the balance.

Many schools commonly sponsor and hold science fairs as one means to help motivate students in science areas. Fairs introduce a hands-on science component to the curriculum, augmenting classroom science instruction. The community-based science fair that we propose shares that rationale, but it incorporates several additional, important components as well. It is not just another science fair.

A community-based science fair enlists the aid of community scientists, teachers, and parents to broaden the students' experiences in science. Not only does this fair aid the school's science instruction, but it also heightens student interest in and excitement about science. The community provides valuable mentoring relationships, presents science in a setting outside of the classroom, and shows vividly the wide spectrum of scientific interests. Because of the breadth of community support, this fair becomes a more important event than could be expected from one based on the school district alone.

OUR SCIENCE FAIR: A BRIEF HISTORY

Eight years ago our local school-community organization decided we should do something to support and enhance our children's science

education. Science was being taught without the hands-on experiences which are not only important to a solid science curriculum, but may also be the single most important element needed to foster a child's love of science. In searching for ways to develop this vital instructional approach, someone suggested that we explore a district-wide science fair that would include our several grade schools and the junior high school. Preparation seemed like a monumental task demanding more than could be expected of teachers alone. However, the size of the project could also be seen as an advantage. Staging a science fair seemed like an excellent way for the community to make a difference in the public education of its children. The problem was that no one knew quite where to begin.

Encouraged by parents from a nearby school district who were producing a science fair in their own community, we borrowed a few notes and outlines and began the lengthy task of designing our own workable system. In that first year, producing our science fair was truly the biggest experiment of all. No one knew if 10 students or 100 would participate. *(Students participate in our fair on a voluntary basis.)* Parents working closely with the school district decided that a joint committee of parents and teachers should be designated as the Science Fair Steering Committee. They designed and distributed fliers, organized a student-parent workshop, and arranged for facilities for the day of the fair. Because awards were considered an important part of the science fair experience, the committee decided that it would have to undertake fund-raising, too; they prepared an advertisement *(ad)* book with contributors from the local business community. The support was very positive, and financial backing was easily obtained.

After months of preparation, the day of project check-in arrived, and so did the students! And they kept arriving. By the time all the participants had set up their projects, there was no room for anyone else! People had to view the projects in shifts. In fact, people were still coming to view projects as they were being dismantled.

We have come a long way since those first days of minimal organization and accompanying chaos. The location and schedule of the fair had to be changed to accommodate all participants. After several years of implementation, evaluation, and revision, the fair now hums with organization and buzzes with excitement. Teams of volunteers host various shifts throughout the day of the fair and the set-up the preceding night. Parents no longer wait for hours while students stand impatiently beside their projects as nervous fidgeting becomes endless boredom. Children look forward to the day of the fair, to displaying their work, and to participating in an event that is certainly one of the most well attended in town.

The judging room is busy but well organized. The display rooms echo the students' anticipation and excitement. Teachers, parents, and principals work side-by-side to produce a science fair where students can proudly display their work and speak with judges and observers about newly learned scientific principles.

WHY HOLD A SCIENCE FAIR AT ALL?

Though the concept of a science fair is not new, not every school or every community has one. And while having a fair does not ensure the existence of a quality school science program, we do believe that it can enhance and reinforce a good program. This is certainly true in elementary schools where students can benefit from experiences in science that supplement the curriculum. Typically, more time and effort in elementary schools is spent on subjects other than science. Even with the best teachers and materials, it is often difficult to bring science alive in the classroom.

A science fair can enhance opportunities for discovery and understanding of science. Creating their own projects and seeing others helps teach students about a variety of experimental techniques. It gives them the chance to experience process skills firsthand. Engaging in a science project requires them to organize, hypothesize, observe, and compare information. They learn to communicate, infer, apply, and draw conclusions while success and recognition serve to enhance their self-esteem.

Such an activity, held outside the classroom, not only reinforces classroom skills and values, but also solidifies intellectual and personal development. This opportunity to have a creative and personal experience with science provides variety to the learning experience as well.

There is also the question of image. How are scientists and the work they do portrayed to our students? Science can look boring and difficult, a subject studied by "stuffy nerds" who don't smile or play and who could not possibly be enjoying their work. Because this image can deter youngsters, we must overcome the stereotype early on. We can do this by giving the students an opportunity to meet with scientists. Through a science fair, students can talk about their projects with scientists who, in turn, can help students realize that what they are learning is important. Such interaction goes far in helping students overcome a fear of science and can change their ideas of what a scientist is like.

WHAT MAKES THIS SCIENCE FAIR UNIQUE?

AN INNOVATIVE SCIENCE FAIR

We are often asked why we chose a fair with community involvement, when the most common type of science fair is school-based. The concept of a school-based science fair is not new; schools and school districts have produced fairs for years. However, community-based science fairs present a fresh slant on this familiar topic. We believe a fair that enlists broad-based community, support, planning and implementation, and which encourages science inquiry and hands-on experimentation by elementary school-aged students is more than just a novel idea. It is, perhaps, the only way to produce such a successful series of events. The fair prospers because of everyone's involvement and commitment to it. Schools alone would find it difficult, if not impossible, to produce all of these activities.

Community-based science fairs send a strong message to our youth. They communicate the importance the school, parents, and community place on good science instruction and programming. They highlight the role of others as teachers of science, and thereby show science as not only a real career choice, but also as a subject worthy of excitement and interest. Students see adults teaming together in an effort to provide them with an experience that is both stimulating and fun at the same time. They see that these adults value science enough to volunteer their time. And, as they do, students learn to view the community as a broader set of teachers who share an interest in student learning.

Throughout this community-based science fair process, science becomes more than a school subject. It comes alive through inquiry and hands-on experimentation. Teachers, parents, scientists, student peers, and other community members serve as teachers in the process and reinforce the importance of science through their personal involvement.

A FAIR FOR EVERYONE

Many people have looked at the science fair experience that we have developed and asked why we start at kindergarten. The key is that young children still believe in magic and are fascinated by the questions science seeks to answer. They have an insatiable desire to understand their world. We have simply capitalized on that interest.

We might better ask of our questioners, "Can we really afford to wait until the junior high or high school years to excite students about science and science inquiry?" With our world becoming more technologically complex with each passing year and with troubling environmental, ethical, and economic issues facing us, the United States cannot afford to have students growing up without a reasonable knowledge and understanding of science. Our students should be literate about concepts and issues, and/or intrigued by their own ability to address them, because of early exposure to good science instruction. Many of these students are tomorrow's leaders, who will be charged with making technical decisions affecting all of us. A population educated in science will make wiser decisions and cast more-informed votes.

A *FAIR* SCIENCE FAIR

The strong desire to create a fair science fair has always been and continues to be of key importance to our community-based fair, just as it will be for yours. It is essential that each student participant receive fair treatment and appropriate feedback. That's why every student should win at the science fair. This can be achieved by presenting everyone with at least a third-place ribbon, certificate award, and public recognition on stage at the awards assembly. Since all of us find motivation in recognition, these awards bolster students' self-image and enhance the positive feelings they have about the fair overall.

However, the competition for awards at the science fair motivates students, too. In order to handle competition as fairly as possible, careful standards are necessary to assure fair and uniform judging. Yet our experience has shown that individual judges can rate the same project differently. They may emphasize different aspects of a project, thereby creating inconsistency in the application of criteria used for assigning awards. On the other hand, some judges naturally score lower than others, even when the relative evaluation of projects is consistent. And, even by teaming two judges together and averaging their scores, consistency among projects may not be achieved. As a result, some truly outstanding projects may not turn out to be winners.

Not Just Another Science Fair addresses these problems. We've developed a set of judging criteria for all judges to follow, thus eliminating the problem of emphasis on different aspects of the project. Our fair uses a computer program to normalize judging team scores, thus avoiding the problem of different scoring levels by judges viewing competing projects. The program goes a step further by providing a means of assigning the awards from these normalized scores. All of these functions are accomplished quickly during the tight schedule of the day of the fair, making it possible to have a fair science fair. (This subject is presented in detail in CHAPTER 4, Producing a Fair Science Fair.)

FOUR EVENTS COMBINE TO CREATE A SUCCESSFUL FAIR

Our fair has evolved into four major events: the Kickoff Assemblies, the Student/Parent Workshop, the actual Science Fair, and post-fair Evaluations. (We have always held our fair on a Saturday in March with project check-in and set-up on the preceding Friday.)

KICKOFF ASSEMBLIES

Classroom teachers are critical in first exciting students about exploring science and participating in a fair. In our fair, their efforts are followed by School Kickoff Assemblies designed to demonstrate to students how to actually conduct a science experiment. An action experiment (usually involving an aspect of physics) is "performed" with the students; they participate in a discussion of variables, observations, data recording, and conclusions.

STUDENT/PARENT WORKSHOP

Within days of the Kickoff Assemblies, the Student/Parent Workshop is held during an evening. A catchy theme and carnival atmosphere convey a sense of fun and excitement to the Workshop. Students and parents observe films on scientific method, participate together in conducting science experiments, and are totally involved with science for a night. Steering Committee members, parents, scientists, and educators conduct mini-group sessions on everything from brainstorming for experiment ideas to experimentation techniques. Students are encouraged to work on team projects for peer support. As with any fair, the parent becomes a resource and encourager for project completion. In addition, a science fair liaison teacher in the school provides support and encouragement.

AT THE FAIR

On the evening preceding the day of the fair, students check in and set up their projects. Previewing the project summaries and reports received from participants the previous week, the Committee has assigned projects to judging teams and now times are selected when they will meet and speak with the judges. *(For details, see CHAPTER 4, Producing a* Fair *Science Fair.)*

On the day of the fair, students are escorted into the project display area when it is their time to speak with the judges. They know their judging time in advance so that they need not arrive more than fifteen minutes prior to judging. However, we have found that students really enjoy the time in the Participants' Activity Room, and some come early just for that. There, they are occupied with films, games, and science-related activities while waiting to be judged. The day concludes with public viewing of the display rooms and an award presentation assembly. During the public viewing, students answer questions and receive comments from community members. Students and visitors alike take on the roles of teachers and learners.

EVALUATION

The fourth event in this fair consists of a post-fair evaluation session held by the Steering Committee. This session has proven very valuable as a means of improving the quality of the fair over the years. At this session, committee members not only share their suggestions, but the evaluation forms circulated the day of the fair are also reviewed.

These four events, plus the refined organization and computer-aided judging, make this science fair unique. Employing the events enhances the ability to create and hold student and parent interest in the science project and fair. In addition, these multiple events help increase the students' exposure to science and a scientific method of investigation.

Compare this organizational plan to a fishing expedition. Classroom teachers initiate the idea for the trip. The Kickoff Assemblies serve as bait; they entice students to become involved in the fair. Students see that science can be fun as they watch dramatic experiments—maybe even with things flying through the air. They learn that a science fair project can pertain to an area of special interest to each of them. These assemblies excite students and encourage them to bring their parents to the Student/Parent Workshop. At that point the hook is set. Support from liaison teachers, parents, and student peers is provided in the critical intervening weeks. Anticipation of the fair, meeting with the judges, receiving ribbons and explaining their projects to visitors allow the Steering Committee to easily reel students in during the final weeks.

THIS BOOK'S ORGANIZATION HELPS YOU ORGANIZE YOUR FAIR

Not Just Another Science Fair explains how and why our unique community-based fair is successful. The following chapters explain the events, organization, and operation of the fair in detail. Feel free to use, modify, or adapt these plans to your particular needs.

Strategies for organizing a large-scale fair are carefully delineated in *CHAPTER 2*, Keeping It All Together. Step-by-step you will move from selecting and forming a Steering Committee through to the post-fair review session. You will find "job" descriptions for the various volunteers and Steering Committee members. Specific timelines are also supplied for planning the fair sufficiently in advance to insure both your success and that of the students.

CHAPTER 3, Science Experiments, is a discussion of how students can apply the scientific method in carrying out their projects, and addresses topic choices for science fair experiments. Projects for the science fair are limited exclusively to experiments in science and engineering. The differences between experiments and demonstrations, inventions, or surveys are also discussed. Tips for planning an experiment, recording data, checking controls, evaluating results, and preparing for one's presentation at the fair are outlined. This unique chapter exposes our bias that science is to be handled and explored, not just studied. Appendix C, Project Ideas, lists science experiments applicable to grades K–8. Some of these projects have a creative twist—in the topic explored, through the method followed, or with the device used for testing.

CHAPTER 4, Producing a *Fair* Science Fair, describes the computer program devised to normalize judging and scores across the judging teams and participants. You will find tips for briefing judges prior to the fair, creating judging criteria, and honoring participants. To make the normalization process more understandable and usable we have made available a copy of the computer program in floppy disk format.

The Appendices contain the *Science Fair Handbook* in its entirety, instructions for fair volunteers, ideas for student projects and Kickoff Assembly projects, and fair forms and fliers. In addition, these forms are included as figures throughout the book. The *Science Fair Handbook* and all of the forms, fliers, letters, and instruction *sheets that you will need for your fair are also on the computer disk. (If you bought this book without a disk, you can still purchase the disk from the store that sold you the book.)* The disk will make it easy for you to use these materials as they are presented or modify them for your own specific needs.

Taken together, these chapters and appendices create a road map for the reader to initiate a *fair* science fair, one which taps the interest and expertise of a community in order to expand students' opportunities in science. Coming next is **not just another science fair**.

2

Order and simplification

are the first steps toward

the mastery of a subject.

Thomas Mann,
The Magic Mountain

KEEPING IT ALL TOGETHER
ORGANIZATION AND EVENTS

■ *The framework for the organization for a community-based science fair is outlined in this chapter and will be helpful as a reference in getting your own fair started. Here you will learn how to set up the Science Fair Steering Committee, how to plan and organize the events, what tasks need to be accomplished, and how to select volunteers to do them. You will also find a time line of events to use to ensure that all tasks are completed on time. Modify these procedures, as needed, to better fit your individual circumstances.*

All of the materials that need to be distributed for the fair are duplicated on the *Not Just Another Science Fair Disk.** The files are in WordPerfect 5.1 format and end with the letters WP. Two typefaces are used–proportional serif and proportional sans serif–in a variety of point sizes. Selecting a Hewlett Packard LaserJet III printer in WordPerfect will reproduce all fonts used. We have included these computer files for your convenience in making changes necessary for your particular circumstances. If you don't have the disk, you can copy the forms from APPENDIX E of this book and write in any information related to your fair. Before going any further, however, let's look at how to get your science fair off the ground.

* If you bought this book without the disk, you can still purchase a disk separately from the store where you bought the book.

HOW TO APPROACH YOUR SCHOOL DISTRICT

Getting started is probably the most challenging part of this, or any other project. Just having the idea and desire to proceed is the first step. The next is trying to convince others, including the local school officials, that it is a worthwhile idea. The superintendent is the first person you must convince in order to produce a community-based science fair. There may be some skepticism as to how this fair will affect the teaching staff, what the educational benefits will be, and what impact the fair will have on school schedules. Present the fair as one in which the parents and community shoulder the organizational burden for its various events and activities. Point to the many ways that the school district can help that will not overtax its staff or resources. *(If the teachers in your district currently sponsor a science fair, the event can only be enhanced by reaching out for community support and involvement.)*

Outline the fair's unique features *(discussed in CHAPTER 1)*. Once the superintendent is convinced of the benefits of a community-based science fair and of the educational benefits for the students, present a plan for reaching all the schools in your district. If a staff member from the district office is unavailable to help, find a teacher or group of teachers who enjoy teaching science and enlist their support. You will most certainly want and need their assistance as you plan activities for the students and parents and distribute materials through the schools.

ESTABLISHING A STEERING COMMITTEE

The Steering Committee is the group that plans and oversees all of the events and activities that comprise the science fair. This group includes administrators, teachers at various grade levels, parents, scientists, a representative of the community's parent group, and other interested members of the community. It is very helpful to have a primary sponsoring community organization *(such as a local PTA, gifted student support group, or other parent group)*. Such an organization can provide a valuable source of volunteers and may provide links to an existing parent/community network.

The fair and its activities should be broken down into many small tasks. This division ensures that each person can have a rather specific *(and not too large)* task to perform. Packaging work in manageable amounts will keep your volunteers from feeling that they have taken on a full-time job by agreeing to assist with the fair.

In order to coordinate all of the tasks and activities given in the time lines discussed later in this chapter, and to keep the workload per person at a reasonable level, we have found it productive to have the responsibilities of Steering Committee members organized as follows.

- Fair Coordinator
- School District Liaison
- Kickoff Assemblies Coordinator
- Volunteer Coordinator
- Student/Parent Workshop Coordinator
- Scientist Judges Coordinator
- Teacher Judges Coordinator
- Set-up and Supply Coordinator
- Participant Activities Coordinator
- Computer Specialist
- Teacher Representatives
- Building Liaison Teachers

The individual roles and responsibilities of each of these committee members are discussed in this chapter, as well as the specific tasks that each member must perform throughout the six months prior to the fair.

STEERING COMMITTEE TASKS

The Steering Committee begins meeting in the early fall to plan for a spring science fair. *(Many districts choose to go on to regional competition and therefore the date of the local fair must be appropriately chosen.)* The Committee meets monthly and divides areas of responsibility suited to members' interests and expediency. *FIGURE 2.1* presents the time line of the four major events that comprise the fair. Subsequent tables present more detailed time lines, first by months prior to the fair, then by weeks before the fair, and finally, by the hour for the 24 hours preceding the fair. These time lines are intended to serve as a comprehensive overview or checklist for all the details that need consideration preparing for and executing the fair. You may need to tailor them to your specific event or to handle your particular needs.

All of the major written materials that are distributed to parents and students throughout the four events of the science fair are summarized in *FIGURE 2.2*. These materials appear again in figures and tables throughout the chapters of this book where they are discussed in detail; they are also on the accompanying computer disk. Of course, any of the fair coordinators can add written material to the event for which she or he has responsibility.

FIGURE 2.1			**MAJOR EVENTS OF THE FAIR**				
SEPT	OCT	NOV	DEC	JAN	FEB	MAR	APR
Establish Steering Committee	Planning	Planning	Planning	Kickoff Assembly	Registration	Set-up	Evaluation
				Student/Parent Workshop		**Day of the Fair!**	

FIGURE 2.2

WRITTEN MATERIAL DISTRIBUTED FOR THE SCIENCE FAIR

WRITTEN MATERIAL NAME	LOCATION	RESPONSIBILITY	DISTRIBUTION TIME
Student/Parent Workshop Fair Announcement Flier	Figure 2.7	Student/Parent Workshop Coordinator	After Kickoff Assemblies, 1 week before the Workshop
Science Fair Handbook Registration Form	Appendix A Figure 2.15	Fair Coordinator	Student/Parent Workshop
Letter to Students Confirming Participation	Figure 2.3	Fair Coordinator	After registration forms are received, 4-5 weeks before the fair
Mailing to Prospective Judges	Figures 4.2, 4.4, 4.5, 4.6 & Appendix A	Scientist & Teacher Judges Coordinators	The week after the Workshop
Community Invitation Flier to Fair	Figure 2.4	Fair Coordinator	One week before the fair
Phone Numbers for Judging Time Information	Figure 2.16	Volunteer Coordinator	Project Check-In the night before the fair
Participants' Booklet Fair Evaluation Form	Figure 2.5 Figure 2.11	Computer Specialist Fair Coordinator	Day of the fair

STEERING COMMITTEE RESPONSIBILITIES

FAIR COORDINATOR

The position of Fair Coordinator, often a community member, has overall responsibility for all aspects of the fair. This position is usually filled by one person, though it can be held by two. Having a Fair Coordinator from the community helps involve parents and others outside of the school. It is easy to allow the schools to take over the fair, but outside involvement is a key to the success of our fair, and every effort should be made to ensure that this involvement is prominent. As with all people associated with the fair *(except the scientist judges)*, the Fair Coordinator need not have a broad science background.

The Fair Coordinator has the overall responsibility of coordinating, initiating, and expediting all of the fair functions. She or

he must ensure that each of the other coordinators on the Steering Committee completes the tasks in a timely and appropriate manner. The Fair Coordinator may have to step in or assist another committee member if there are difficulties as the fair date approaches. Time and material management is a major part of this job.

The Fair Coordinator chairs all Steering Committee meetings, prepares agendas, takes notes/minutes at each meeting, and follows up on all unresolved problems after the meetings. The Fair Coordinator is also responsible for overseeing the preparation of all of the letters and printed material that are sent out to the school district, Steering Committee, or students, and serves as the liaison to the school district.

Together with the Set-up and Supply Coordinator, the Fair Coordinator is responsible for preparing the display area table layout in early February once the registrations are completed. The Fair Coordinator is present during project check-in and general fair set-up on the night before the day of the fair. Also, the Fair Coordinator is responsible for delivering the lists of judging times to the parent volunteers.

The Fair Coordinator is present at the fair to see that all runs smoothly. She or he should check on the timely arrival of volunteers, be available to assist and answer questions, and make last-minute changes, decisions, substitutions, and so on, as needed. Usually the Fair Coordinator oversees score checking and award distribution and assists during the Awards Ceremony. The Fair Coordinator, as well as other Steering Committee coordinator members, should obtain assistance as needed in meeting his/her responsibilities.

The Fair Coordinator is responsible for:
- chairing Steering Committee meetings
- modifying the *Science Fair Handbook (APPENDIX A)*
- modifying the letter to students confirming registration *(FIGURE 2.3)*
- modifying the flier inviting the community *(FIGURE 2.4)*
- assisting the Set-up and Supply Coordinator with the table layout
- previewing and sorting of project summaries and reports *(see CHAPTER 4)*
- overseeing project check-in Friday night
- assigning judges and judging times
- delivering judging times to parent volunteers

FIGURE 2.3　**LETTER TO STUDENT CONFIRMING PARTICIPATION**

March 1, 1999

Dear Science Fair Participant:

This letter is to confirm your participation in the Science Fair scheduled for Saturday, March 13, 1999. Below, we have listed several important reminders for that day:

1.　Friday, March 12, is set-up and check-in. Please arrive at the school with your project between 5 and 7 p.m. *NO LATE SET-UP WILL BE ALLOWED.*

2.　Judging will begin at 9:15 a.m. Saturday morning. There will be special activities in the gym for participants waiting to be judged.

3.　We will have phone numbers available if you wish to call Saturday morning to find out what time you will be judged. Please arrive 15 minutes prior to your scheduled judging time.

4.　The fair will be open to the public from 1:30 to 3:00 p.m. on Saturday. We encourage you to stand by your project so you can answer questions for the public.

5.　You are to write your own project summary. Make sure you answer the questions that were listed in the *Science Fair Handbook*. A copy of those pages is attached. *YOUR PROJECT SUMMARY WILL BE DUE THE MONDAY BEFORE THE FAIR. PLEASE GIVE IT TO YOUR LIAISON TEACHER ON MONDAY, MARCH 8 BEFORE 3:00 P.M.*

　　You will be given a copy of your title page as your receipt. You will NOT have to bring another copy of your paper to the fair.

6.　The decision of the judges is final.

7.　Questions about rules? Contact your school liaison teacher.

FIGURE 2.4   **SCIENCE FAIR COMMUNITY INVITATION FLIER**

A
SCIENCE
FAIR
INVITATION

The entries are on the starting line!
The BIG day has finally arrived...

The VALLEY DISTRICT
SCIENCE FAIR

Saturday, March 13, 1999
Public Viewing 1:30–3:00 p.m.

SEE THE BEST JUNIOR SCIENTISTS
GO FOR THE BLUE !

Awards Presentation
3:00–3:20 p.m.
Junior High Gym

SCHOOL DISTRICT LIAISON

This person should be an administrator or teacher, employed by the district, who is willing to help organize the fair. The School District Liaison must be able to win the assistance and cooperation of other school district personnel, communicate with teachers and principals, and report to the superintendent. She or he arranges for liaison teachers in each school and makes sure they are familiar with fair rules and procedures. Activities coordinated at the district level can include table set-up, custodial services, duplicating, typing or word processing, securing clipboards for judges, circulating materials, arranging for facilities, and ordering awards and ribbons, to name just a few.

If your district is willing to contribute to the expense of the fair, purchasing awards and certificates, providing duplication of materials, and donating postage is a good way to help. However, since funds needed for the fair are rather small, they can be raised with contributions from the local community if the district is unwilling or unable to contribute. For example, in our district, parents obtained funds for one fair by selling advertisements in the *Science Fair Participants' Booklet* to local merchants. Local businesses participated by placing ads in the booklet that listed the names of student participants. A sample page from the booklet showing both students' names and advertisements is shown in *FIGURE 2.5.*

In our school district, the School District Liaison is responsible for purchasing awards. All students entering the science fair should receive a first-, second-, or third-place ribbon. In addition, projects receiving first-place awards should be considered for an Outstanding Award; winners receive a medallion or lapel pin in addition to a special purple ribbon. Your school district can also print certificates of participation for all students to be given out at each school's awards day later in the year.

The School District Liaison also has students make construction-paper versions of the ribbons to be distributed the day of the fair during Public Viewing. This allows us to save the actual ribbons for the Awards Ceremony.

The School District Liaison is responsible for:
> ‣ duplicating, typing, and distributing printed materials *(including mailings)*

FIGURE 2.5   **PAGE FROM THE *SCIENCE FAIR PARTICIPANTS' BOOKLET***

1ST GRADE
SCIENCE
PROJECTS

#101
Smith, Jessica
Which Paper Towel Is Strongest?

#102
Jones, Jimmy
Which Airplane Flies Best?

#103
Walker, Susan
How Does Cigarette Smoke Affect Plants?

#104
Warner, John
Young, Rich
Bouncing Balls

#105
Kelly, Cheryl
Which Light Is Best for Plants?

- informing other school personnel about science fair activities
- preparing construction-paper versions of ribbons
- ordering and preparing awards and certificates
- arranging dates for Kickoff Assemblies within the various schools
- preparing press releases for the workshop and the fair
- briefing each school's liaison teachers
- collecting and processing all science fair registration forms
- ordering and preparing awards and certificates

KICKOFF ASSEMBLIES COORDINATOR

This person, usually a parent from the community, arranges the school assemblies to announce the upcoming science fair. A dazzling science experiment is presented, and the students participate in all aspects of it–in other words, the assemblies are a key motivator to spur participation in the upcoming fair.

The coordinator can prepare the format for the assemblies or allow the presenters to do so. The number of presenters needed will depend on the size of your district and the time commitment needed from each presenter. Assemblies are most effective when they are designed for 100–150 students. Larger groups make individual participation difficult, and getting students excited and involved in the hands-on fun of science is key to the success of the program. The coordinator may also want to attend all of the Kickoff Assemblies, acting as moderator.

The experiments performed at the assemblies should be geared to the students' level. We have used three divisions of presentations: kindergarten through 3rd grade, 4th through 6th grade, and junior high school. Sample Kickoff Assembly experiments for each grade division are offered in *APPENDIX D.*

The Kickoff Assemblies Coordinator is responsible for:
- designating the school schedule
- designing the experiment for the Kickoff Assemblies *(see APPENDIX D)*
- preparing the materials, equipment, and supplies for the assemblies
- presenting the assemblies

VOLUNTEER COORDINATOR

The Volunteer Coordinator finds volunteers and instructs each of them as to what tasks they will perform on the day and evening of the fair set-up and the fair day itself. *FIGURE 2.6* summarizes who is needed on the weekend of the fair. *(The numbers shown work well for a fair with 150–200 participants.)* Details of the various tasks to be performed by each volunteer are listed in *APPENDIX B.* These guide lists should be given by the coordinator to each volunteer; they can be modified to fit your specific location, project division, and so on. Job commitments should be kept to two or three hours at the most. Parents whose children will be participating in the fair are usually more than willing to assist. Reminder postcards should be sent out to the volunteers about one week before the fair to verify the time commitment and the place and time of arrival.

The Volunteer Coordinator also finds helpers for the Student/Parent Workshop. He or she is responsible for producing the flier, "Attention All Parents and Junior Scientists," which is a brief list of people to telephone on the morning of the fair to find out the specific judging time for each student. *(See FIGURE 2.16.)*

The Volunteer Coordinator is responsible for:

- ▸ contacting all volunteers to assist with:
  The Student/Parent Workshop
  Set-up on the day before the fair
  Friday night project check-in
  The fair

STUDENT/PARENT WORKSHOP COORDINATOR

The Student/Parent Workshop Coordinator is in charge of producing an effective workshop, a critical event in the overall success of the fair. His or her responsibilities include selecting a workshop theme that will generate enthusiasm for the fair and finding an appropriate site. The Workshop Coordinator also oversees the selection of activities for the workshop, preparation of decorations, coordination of parent volunteers, preparation and distribution of handouts.

FIGURE 2.6	**VOLUNTEER FUNCTIONS THE WEEKEND OF THE FAIR**		
TASK	TIME	NUMBER OF VOLUNTEERS	APPENDIX B, FORM
Facility set-up	Fri., 3:15 p.m.–5:00 p.m.	6	3
Project check-in & set-up	Fri., 5:00 p.m.–7:00 p.m.	6	4
Final set-up	Fri., 7:00 p.m.–9:00 p.m.	6	5
Parents receiving home calls	Sat., 7:45 a.m.– 8:45 a.m.	5	6
Student check-in	Sat., 9:00 a.m.–11:00 a.m.	2	7
Participants' activities	Sat., 9:00 a.m.–12:00 noon	10	8
Students' escorts	Sat., 9:00 a.m.–11:30 a.m.	4	10
General traffic control	Sat., 9:00 a.m.–12:00 noon Sat., 1:00 p.m.–3:00 p.m.	3 2	
Information table	Sat., 8:30 a.m.–10:30 a.m. Sat., 10:30 a.m.–12:30 p.m. Sat., 12:30 p.m.–2:30 p.m.	1 1 1	9
Award distribution	Sat., 1:15 p.m.– 2:15 p.m.	4	11
Clean-up	Sat., 3:20 p.m.–3:30 p.m.	4	12

The flier announcing the Workshop is the first written information that students and parents receive about the fair *(FIGURE 2.7)*. It is distributed after the Kickoff Assemblies and includes a list of project ideas *(APPENDIX C)*.

The Student/Parent Workshop Coordinator is responsible for:

- selecting the workshop theme and location *(APPENDIX B, FORM 1)*
- organizing the workshop events
- preparing a flier announcing the workshop *(FIGURE 2.7)*
- coordinating volunteers for the evening

An example of a workshop format appears in *FIGURE 2.8.*

FIGURE 2.7 **STUDENT/PARENT WORKSHOP AND SCIENCE FAIR ANNOUNCEMENT FLIER**

WE HEAR HE IS A WONDERFUL WIZ-
IF EVER A WIZ THERE WAS

PALS / DISTRICT 44

SCIENCE FAIR
COMING
MARCH 12

**If you have ever wondered about
the workings of a *WIZARD OF SCIENCE*,
students and parents will want to follow
our Yellow Brick Road *TOGETHER* to**

THE WIZARD'S WORKSHOP
VALLEY VIEW JUNIOR HIGH SCHOOL CAFETERIA
Tuesday, January 12, 6:30 p.m.

KINDERGARTEN–8TH-GRADE STUDENTS

Meet our Wizard, **DR. WILLIS**, Professor of Engineering at the University of
Illinois at Chicago, as he performs **SCIENCE MAGIC**.

Then stop at the **SCARECROW'S BRAINSTORMING TABLE** where teachers, parents,
and scientists will help you choose a project.

And, as you walk through the **FIELD OF POPPIES**, you will see all of the stages of
actual experiments on display. Be sure to try one.

Next, you can see a movie: **BYRON BLACKBEAR AND THE SCIENTIFIC METHOD**.

There will be a display of **LIBRARY BOOKS** for you to look through.

We will take you through **RECORDING YOUR RESULTS** using our very simple method.

Last, you will follow the Yellow Brick Road to the **EMERALD CITY** for any additional
questions that you may have about the Science Fair.

THEN YOU WILL CLICK YOUR HEELS THREE TIMES AND SAY GOODNIGHT.

Younger brothers and sisters can play in supervised **MUNCHKINLAND**
during the Workshop.

FIGURE 2.8 **COMMITTEE OUTLINE FOR STUDENT/PARENT WORKSHOP**

SCIENCE FAIR STUDENT/PARENT WORKSHOP

VALLEY JUNIOR HIGH SCHOOL

TUESDAY, JAN. 12, 1999, 6:30-8:30 p.m.

THEME: **The Science Wizard of Oz**

LOCATION: **Valley Junior High School**

ROOM: **Cafeteria, hallway, and nearby classrooms**

COORDINATOR: **Mrs. Sands, 555–1234**

Arrival: *Science Fair Handbooks* and registration forms will be distributed at the welcome table. Visitors will be directed to follow the "Yellow Brick Road" to the cafeteria.

Lead-off Speaker: The evening will begin with a presentation by Dr. J. W. Willis, Professor of Engineering at the University of Illinois at Chicago. He will be performing an experiment for the benefit of students and parents. His presentation will last 30–45 minutes.

Announcements: When his presentation is complete, Ms. Smith, Principal of School #2, will welcome the visitors and make announcements regarding science fair rules, procedures, and the evening's events.

Special Arrangements for Young Children: Younger siblings may be left in "Munchkinland," which will be supervised by two parent volunteers. The "Munchkins" will watch *The Wizard of Oz* movie while parents accompany their older children on their journey through Oz.

A JOURNEY THROUGH OZ

1.   **First stop:** Students meet the Scarecrow and are given an opportunity to speak informally with our volunteers who will be positioned at tables in the rear of the cafeteria. Visitors may ask questions regarding the scientific method, experimental ideas, designing experiments, or anything pertaining to the actual experiments.

TABLE 1	TABLE 2	TABLE 3
K–3	4–5	6–8
Mr. Webb	Mr. Edwards	Mr. Foster
Ms. Adams	Mrs. Mack	Ms. Collins

FIGURE 2.8 *continued*

2.   **Second stop:** Students will follow the yellow brick road to the "Field of Poppies" where they will view the steps of experiments from set-up to recording results. Two volunteers will be there to answer questions about the experiments and to assist students in trying parts of the experiments. In addition, signs will display both scientific jargon and layman's terms for each phase of the experiment as follows:

PURPOSE: **What is the question I want to answer?**
HYPOTHESIS: **What do I predict will happen?**
PROCEDURE: **What will I do to answer my question?**
MANIPULATED VARIABLE: **What am I going to change?**
RESPONDING VARIABLE: **What happens as a result of what I change?**
CONTROLS: **What things do I keep the same?**
RESULTS: **What happened and what does it mean?**
CONCLUSION: **What is the answer to my question?**

This display will be set up in the hallway near the cafeteria for easy traffic flow.
     VOLUNTEERS: Ms. Parker, Mr. Jenkins

3.   **Third Stop:** Students will follow the "Yellow Brick Road" to see the movie *Byron Blackbear and the Scientific Method (Coronet Films, Deerfield, Illinois).*

4.   **Fourth Stop:** Students will follow the "Yellow Brick Road" to a display of books relating to science fair projects in the library room. A person from the local library's Young People's Department will be present to answer questions regarding the books. He or she will provide a listing of the books to make it easier for students to find them at a later date. In addition, every school will provide a number of books from their libraries. Allow students to check out books that evening or at least reserve them if actual check-out is not possible.

5.   **Fifth Stop:** Students will follow the "Yellow Brick Road" to the RESULTS ROOM where sample worksheets will be handed out for recording results.

6.   **Sixth Stop:** Students will follow the "Yellow Brick Road" to the Emerald City which will be lit with a green floodlight. We will have a wizard there who will say goodnight to all. There will be helpers from the Committee there to answer last-minute questions regarding the fair. Last: click heels three times and go home!
     VOLUNTEERS: Mrs. Bonn, Mr. Young

SCIENTIST JUDGES COORDINATOR

Judging is performed by teams of two, each consisting of an educator and a scientist. The educator should be someone very familiar with the performance capabilities of the grade level being judged. The scientist judges are asked in advance of the day of the fair what grade level they prefer to judge. Every attempt is made to honor the preferences.

The Scientist Judges Coordinator must contact people with a scientific or engineering background who are potential judges for the fair. The first source for these judges is your own community, parents, and friends. High school science teachers make excellent scientist judges for an elementary school fair. Many scientists enjoy judging fairs and you will find them willing to give their time.

The Coordinator attends and contributes to Steering Committee meetings and modifies material to be mailed to potential judges. However, judges cannot be contacted until the final number of participants is confirmed; the deadline for submitting project entry forms is six weeks before the day of the fair. At this time, the maximum number of judges needed can be established and information is mailed to the previously contacted judges. A sample judging invitation letter and instructions for judges appear in *CHAPTER 4*, Producing a *Fair* Science Fair, in *FIGURES 4.2, 4.4, 4.5,* and *4.6,* all of which are mailed to the judges along with *APPENDIX A*. Typically, judges are assigned between five and nine projects, with seven to nine being preferable for fairness in scoring. The Scientist Judges Coordinator usually has to spend some time on the telephone a few days before the fair, tracking down the last few judges needed as a consequence of cancellations. Therefore, it is advisable to ask one or two judges to fill in as emergency judges the day of the fair.

The Scientist Judges Coordinator is responsible for:
- contacting scientists willing to judge at the fair
- modifying and organizing mailings to potential judges

TEACHER JUDGES COORDINATOR

The tasks of this coordinator are very similar to the Scientist Judges Coordinator. The Teacher Judges Coordinator should probably be a teacher. He or she should recruit other teachers to be teacher judges at the fair. We have found that elementary- and middle-school teachers are best suited. However, we do not recommend that you use teachers from your own district. Teachers within the district have been involved with development of student projects, and they know many of the students through general classroom instruction. Instead, select judges from neighboring grade school districts and from parents and other community members who are in the field of grade school education. If you choose to use teacher judges from your own district, consider having them judge a grade lower than what they teach to avoid the problem of student familiarity.

The Teacher Judges Coordinator is responsible for:
- contacting teachers willing to judge for the fair
- modifying and organizing mailings to potential judges

SET-UP AND SUPPLY COORDINATOR

This person is responsible for overseeing the setting up of tables and gathering the supplies for the fair check-in on Friday evening before the Saturday fair. This coordinator prepares the table layout, works closely with the School District Liaison to obtain necessary tables, directs the placement of the tapes and labels, locates directional signs throughout the school, and sees that check-in tables and Participants' Activities Room tables are set up correctly. The coordinator must gather the appropriate supplies, but the bulk of the work occurs from Friday 3:00 p.m. until 5:00 p.m. before project check-in begins. This position is a good choice for a volunteer with limited time available.

Tables needed to support student project displays may be borrowed from other schools. The tables should be delivered to the fair site by Friday afternoon. Cafeteria tables work very well for the project display area.

Projects are grouped on tables in order of project number, and tables are arranged in the room by grade level. *(See APPENDIX A for specific project size limits.)* We have found it convenient to assign each grade level a color corresponding to available colored tape and colored computer file labels *(see APPENDIX B, Form 3)*. A strip of colored tape is placed along the front edge of the table behind which a student project will be displayed. *(Gym tape is the product of choice because it is so easy to remove.)* A computer-printed project identification label is placed on the tape *(see FIGURE 2.9)*. This practice facilitates clean-up and label removal by simply pulling up the colored tape.

The use of computer-generated labels is invaluable in the organization of materials at the science fair. Ten identification labels are printed for each student in the fair. One of these labels is placed on the colored tape to designate the location for each student's project. All of the labels are generated by the Computer Specialist. The uses of the other nine labels are discussed in the section on the tasks of the Computer Specialist.

The Set-up and Supply Coordinator is also responsible for the set-up of all other rooms used including the Participants' Activities Room, the Judges' Room, and the stage area where the awards are presented. Depending on the school district's involvement, there may be custodial help as well. Set-up for check-in should be completed before 5:00 p.m. on the night before the fair.

The Set-up and Supply Coordinator is responsible for:
- preparing the table layout *(in conjunction with the Fair Coordinator)* for Friday night check-in and the Saturday fair
- organizing the set-up of all the rooms for the fair, including the Judges' Room and the Participants' Activity Room
- gathering supplies such as colored tape, labels, name tags for judges and volunteers, and directional signs

PARTICIPANTS' ACTIVITIES COORDINATOR

This person is the director of the Participants' Activity Room, an area planned to provide science-related activities, including computer games and videos, for students to enjoy while they wait for their judging time. Students can enjoy this time rather than becoming nervous *(or bored)* before speaking to the judges. In fact, we have found that some students deliberately come to the fair early or stay late just to be involved in these activities. At other fairs, participants customarily wait at their projects for judging. This can be tedious for young students as well as noisy for judging. At our fair, the Participants' Activities Room provides a supervised and constructive alternative to that practice while keeping the project display areas quiet for judging. The room should be open and available to all participants throughout the morning of the fair.

The Participant Activities Coordinator is responsible for all functions in this room on the day of the fair. She or he can be either a teacher or parent. Specific responsibilities include planning the morning's activities, coordinating with the Set-up and Supply Coordinator for supplies and room set-up, and working with the Volunteer Coordinator to obtain volunteers to work there *(see APPENDIX B, Form 8)*.

Usually a large room like a gym or cafeteria is used because it can accommodate several activities for various grade levels. Most often there will be films, magazines, or books provided by the library, at least two tables of craft-type activities, computers, and some large motor-skill activities. There must be several parent volunteers, as this room can become quite crowded and busy. There should be a microphone for announcing the names of students as they are to be judged and a blackboard so their names can be written. *(Sometimes younger children get so busy that they forget why they are there, so it is important to be persistent in trying to locate them. One of the pre-printed labels is used as a name tag, since it provides another way to locate a distracted child who doesn't hear his or her name called.)*

The Participants' Activities Coordinator is responsible for:
- planning all activities for the room the day the fair
- preparing lists of supplies needed for the activities
- preparing table and equipment layout for that room
- organizing and coordinating volunteers during that time

COMPUTER SPECIALIST

A computer data base is invaluable for handling all of the registration information. The Computer Specialist is someone who can work with available data base computer software to input the name, address, telephone number, project title, school, grade, teacher's name, and partner's name, if any, for each participant. This person is also responsible for producing the labels that are used to identify all of the student materials for the fair. The label contains the student's name, project title, and project number. The labels are color-coded by grade level (see the sample in FIGURE 2.9).

Projects are numbered as follows: Kindergarten projects are 001, 002, 003, and so on; first-grade projects are 101, 102, 103, and so on, up to eighth-grade projects, which are numbered 801, 802, 803, and so on. Ten labels are needed for each student participating in the fair. The data base should allow sorting the projects by grade level and alphabetizing the names within each grade level. The best format for producing the labels is to have all 10 labels for each student grouped together, with all the projects at a grade level grouped together, and the project labels ordered alphabetically within each grade level. This order makes finding the labels easy and efficient during project check-in the night before the fair and student check-in the morning of the fair. If two students participate as a team on a project, each student should have a full set of labels printed. If the team participants are at different grade levels, the project should be grouped with the higher of the grade levels, as that is how it will be judged. Labels are printed the week before the fair after project summaries/reports are submitted. Thus, labels are printed only for those projects that are actually completed and entered in the fair. Use file folder labels because of their convenient size (5/8 x 3 inches) and their availability in colors. Distribute them according to FIGURE 2.10.

FIGURE 2.9	COMPUTER LABEL

#101   Andrews, Susan   Grade 1

How does temperature affect the life of a battery?

FIGURE 2.10	USE OF STUDENT IDENTIFICATION LABELS	
LOCATION	PLACEMENT	TOTAL
2 per Judging Sheet	Upper left corner & Comment Section	4
Display Table	On tape	1
Project Summary/Report	Upper right corner	1
Project Display	Upper right corner	1
Judging Tally Sheet	In order of judging time	1
Name Tag	On student	1
Awards List	In order of award by grade level	1

In addition to labels, the Computer Specialist produces check-in sheets from the data base to be used for project check-in the night before the fair. The same data base is used to produce the Science Fair Participants' Booklet which lists the names and project titles for all the students in the fair. *(The booklet also contains a Science Fair Evaluation Form, FIGURE 2.11, and any ads which may have been sold to support the fair.)* It is distributed with the students' construction-paper awards the day of the fair. *(See FIGURE 2.5 for a sample page from the Science Fair Participants' Booklet.)*

The Computer Specialist should also have responsibility for the computer program FAIR, which is used for processing judges' scores and assigning awards. *(The program is described in detail in CHAPTER 4, Producing a Fair Science Fair.)* The specialist may also be the presenter at the Judges' Workshop and works with the Scientist and Teacher Judges Coordinators to answer judges' questions.

The Computer Specialist is responsible for:
- preparing the list of all science fair participants
- printing labels to use for student/project identification
- operating the computer program FAIR to assign awards
- preparing the Participants' Booklet *(FIGURE 2.5)*

FIGURE 2.11   **SCIENCE FAIR EVALUATION FORM**

1.   What can we do to make next year's science fair better?

2.   What was the best part of the science fair?

3.   Would you like to help with next year's science fair? *(circle one)*

          YES   NO

4.   If the answer is YES, please provide the following information:

      Name

      Address

      Phone

      THANK YOU!

TEACHER REPRESENTATIVES

The Steering Committee should include teachers from primary, intermediate, and junior-high grades so you can ensure that the materials and activities presented will always be age-appropriate and an enhancement to the curriculum. These teachers serve as advisors to the Committee and are very important to the entire planning process. Their communication with their colleagues is critical to the planning and implementation of the fair. The Teacher Representatives on the Steering Committee can certainly help the School District Liaison find liaison teachers in each of the schools in the district.

BUILDING LIAISON TEACHERS

Each school building in the school district should have a teacher liaison who interacts with the Steering Committee through the Teacher Representatives. The Building Liaison Teachers are not necessarily members of the Steering Committee, but their efforts are invaluable in working with the science fair participants to ensure that their projects are safe, that students are receiving whatever guidance is needed at home, and that their questions are answered about fair procedures, policies, scientific methods, and so on. *(We found in our district that the Committee became too large if all of the Building Liaison Teachers were included, but interested people are always welcome at Steering Committee meetings.)* Specific Building Liaison Teacher duties are listed below.

The Building Liaison Teachers are responsible for:
- reviewing student registration forms
  Were the rules followed?
  Is the form legible?
  Is a partner properly identified?
  Does the student need some school/community assistance in designing the project?
- making copies of registration forms and sending originals to the Fair Coordinator
- assuring that the experiments will be conducted safely and that use of animals is carefully restricted to behavioral observations according to the rules *(See APPENDIX A.)*

- being available to assist and advise student participants. Check with students regularly *(once per week is desirable)* during the approximately six-week time period between registration and the weekend of the fair
- notifying the Fair Coordinator of all cancellations
- volunteering to assist at the fair, if possible

PUTTING TOGETHER ALL OF THE PLAYERS

Now that we have covered the tasks of the people who will produce the four fair events, we will explain how all of their efforts come together to present a successful school-community science fair experience for your students. Beginning with the Kickoff Assemblies, we will show you how each person fits into the collage of exciting activities to stimulate students' interest in science. The time lines that follow *(FIGURE 2.12 and 2.13)* guide you step-by-step through the entire planning process for your science fair.

FIGURE 2.12

TIME LINE OF EVENTS AND RESPONSIBILITIES
Seven to Two Months Before the Fair

OVERSITE GROUP	SEPT	OCT	NOV	DEC	JAN WK 1	JAN WK 2	JAN WK 3	JAN WK 4
Steering Committee	Set site and date of fair	Hold first planning meeting; confirm site and date of fair	Meet to review Workshop and assemblies	Meet to review Workshop and assemblies				
District	Order awards and certificates	Select liaison teachers	Meet with liaison teachers	Print Handbook		Order certificates	Make paper ribbons; confirm fair site	Prepare press release for fair
Student/ Parent Workshop Coordinator	Find location; select theme	Arrange activities	Design flier and press release		Issue press release		Event occurs; distribute Handbook	
Kickoff Assemblies Coordinator		Select theme	Find presenters	Design presentation		Assemblies presented;distribute Workshop flier and list of projects (Appendix C)		
Fair Coordinator	Revise Handbook as needed			Prepare letter confirming student participation				Prepare flier inviting community to fair
Scientist Judges Coordinator					Contact possible judges			
Teacher Judges Coordinator					Contact possible judges			
Computer Specialist								
Participant Activities Coordinator					Plan activities and order supplies			
Volunteer Coordinator					Find helpers for Student/Parent Workshop			

FIGURE 2.13

TIME LINE OF EVENTS AND RESPONSIBILITIES
Two Months Before the Fair

DUTY	FEB WK 1	FEB WK 2	FEB WK 3	FEB WK 4	MAR WK 1	MAR WK 2	FRIDAY 3 - 5 p.m.	FRIDAY 5 - 7 p.m.	FRIDAY 7 - 9 p.m.	FRIDAY 9 p.m.
Steering Committee	Registration forms due; review forms					Project Preview (Appendix B, Form 2)			Judges preview projects - optional (Appendix B, Form 5)	
District			Arrange for table set-up		Send home Invitation Flier to fair	Arrange for clipboards for judges				
Fair Coordinator							Project check-in (Appendix B, Form 4)	Review and assign projects to judges (Appendix B, Form 5)	Deliver judging time lists to parent volunteers (Appendix B, Form 6)	
Scientist Judges Coordinator	Send letters to Judges				Confirm Judges					
Teacher Judges Coordinator	Send letters to Judges				Confirm Judges					
Computer Specialist	Enter names in data base		Prepare Participants' Booklet			Prepare student labels & check-in list				
Participant Activity Coordinator	Finalize site and supply arrangements									
Volunteer Coordinator	Contact Volunteers for set-up, check-in and fair									
Set-up/ Supply Coordinator					Gather supplies for check-in and fair	Prepare table layout	Set-up for check-in and fair (Appendix B, Form 3)			

SCIENCE FAIR EVENTS

Now let's look in detail at each aspect of the fair itself. Of the four major science fair events, the initial two, the Kickoff Assemblies and the Student/Parent Workshop, are the key activities that set everyone buzzing about the coming fair. During these events, students are introduced to the principles of scientific discovery. They review elements of an experiment in simple terms and then learn to apply these elements to hands-on experiments. Both events are designed to be entertaining and educational. Students have several opportunities to be involved, to do experiments, and to have fun while learning. The third event of the fair is, of course, the science fair itself. Last is the evaluation, which begins the day of the fair and concludes at a final Steering Committee meeting the following month.

EVENT 1: THE KICKOFF ASSEMBLIES

The Kickoff Assemblies are held in each school in the district about eight weeks before the fair. Their purpose is to motivate students about experimentation in science, to lead into the coming Student/Parent Workshop, and, of course, to announce the fair itself. In order to present assemblies that are age-appropriate, consider three grade groupings, such as K–3, 4–6, and 7–8. *(You may need to alter this format depending on your schools.)*

We've discovered that the most successful format for motivating students is one that involves them in participating in all phases of an experiment on a simple but fun topic. Kickoff Assembly experiments should use a large portion of the staging area so that all students in the audience can get a feeling for the activity. *(Sample assembly experiments appear in APPENDIX D.)* Experiments involving physics with things that speed, spin, fly, or hurtle across the room are definitely the most popular. Though usually rather simple, the experiments should always use materials that students can find in their homes or garages. Students must not feel that only topics worthy of Nobel Prizes are worth entering.

The entire assembly lasts about 30 minutes. Students are encouraged to participate and discover along with the Coordinator. First, the Coordinator displays a large wall chart which itemizes the

| FIGURE 2.14 | **KICKOFF ASSEMBLIES EXPERIMENT CHART** |

QUESTION	HYPOTHESIS	VARIABLES	CONTROL	CONCLUSIONS
What is the question I want to answer?	What do I predict will happen?	Manipulated: What am I going to change? Responding: What happens as a result of what I change?	What things do I keep the same?	What is the answer to my question?

major elements in an experiment and refers to it during the discussion (see FIGURE 2.14).

In order to fill in the chart at the lower grades, the Coordinator asks students to select the matching statements about the experiment from a group of statements printed on construction paper. First, they select the question by reviewing the materials provided to do the experiment *(Step 1, Select a Question)*.* They then determine the hypothesis, their best guess as to what the experiment will show *(Step 2, Form a Hypothesis)*. The Coordinator also asks students to select the manipulated and responding variables as well as controls. For the primary students, the chart is used in conjunction with the following questions:

QUESTION: **What is the question I want to answer?**

HYPOTHESIS: **What do I predict will happen?**

MANIPULATED VARIABLE: **What am I going to change?**

RESPONDING VARIABLE: **What happens as a result of what I change?**

CONTROLS: **What things do I keep the same?**

CONCLUSION: **What is the answer to my question?**

The Coordinator selects students to assist with the performance of the experiment. They help by holding equipment, making measurements, and overseeing the project.

* The "steps" mentioned in this section refer to those outlined in FIGURE 3.1.

The Coordinator does not assign anyone to record data yet. Students quickly see that they cannot recall all the information, and they readily understand the need to keep logs and records of their work. Then the group performs the experiment with at least three different trials. The Coordinator discusses the need for repeating the experiment to show that an answer is not simply accidental or the result of an error. The students in the primary grades then select from among the trials the number which best represents their results. Intermediate and junior-high students average the results *(Step 3, Perform the Experiment)*. At the direction of the students in each group, the Coordinator draws a graph on an overhead projector, showing the results *(Step 4, Prepare the Results)*. They discuss results and possible sources of error as well as ways to improve or change the experiment *(Step 5, Explain the Results)*. They fill in the conclusion on the wall chart and compare it with their hypothesis *(Step 6, Draw Conclusions)*. It is important that the Kickoff Assemblies be exciting and that the Student/Parent Workshop follow soon afterwards. The spirit of enthusiasm generated in the assemblies will then carry over to the Student/Parent Workshop. Before leaving the assemblies, the students are reminded to watch for information about the upcoming science fair and Student/Parent Workshop. After the assemblies, all of the schools should send home fliers announcing the workshop and the fair. A short list of possible topics for experiments from *APPENDIX C* can be attached to the flier to assist students in selecting a project.

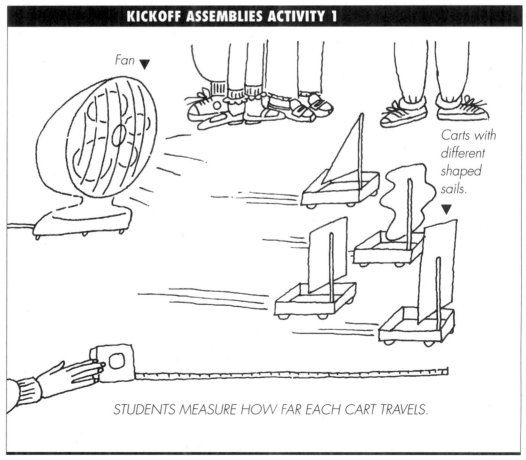

KICKOFF ASSEMBLIES ACTIVITY 1

Fan ▼

Carts with different shaped sails. ▼

STUDENTS MEASURE HOW FAR EACH CART TRAVELS.

KICKOFF ASSEMBLIES ACTIVITY 2

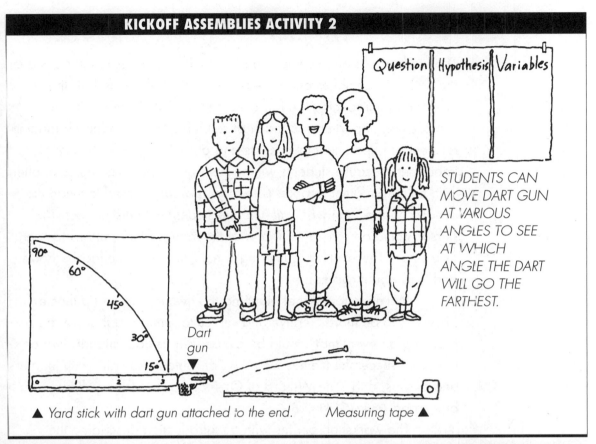

Question | Hypothesis | Variables

STUDENTS CAN MOVE DART GUN AT VARIOUS ANGLES TO SEE AT WHICH ANGLE THE DART WILL GO THE FARTHEST.

90°
60°
45°
30°
15°

Dart gun

▲ Yard stick with dart gun attached to the end.

Measuring tape ▲

KICKOFF ASSEMBLIES ACTIVITY 3

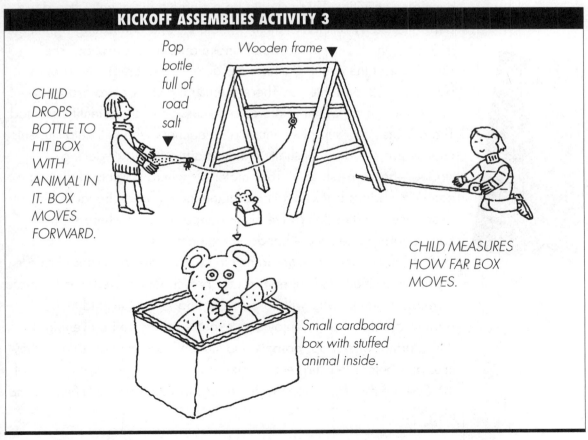

Pop bottle full of road salt ▼

Wooden frame ▼

CHILD DROPS BOTTLE TO HIT BOX WITH ANIMAL IN IT. BOX MOVES FORWARD.

CHILD MEASURES HOW FAR BOX MOVES.

Small cardboard box with stuffed animal inside.

EVENT 2: THE STUDENT/PARENT WORKSHOP

The workshop is an evening event held within a week to ten days after the Kickoff Assemblies and at least six weeks before the fair. In addition to introducing the fair concept to parents, the workshop provides an opportunity to teach or reinforce steps used in performing a scientific experiment to students and parents together. This is important, because students will be doing their projects at home, often with help from other people. *(The term "parent" is used to mean the out-of-school person who will help the student with the project. This person could be a relative, friend of the family, older family member, or mentor.)* This evening gathering is held at one of the local schools and lasts about two hours.

We have found that planning the evening around a theme allows us to be more creative and serves to remind us that we are planning an event that should be fun as well as educational. Two of our more successful themes were "A Fair Before the Fair" with jugglers and clowns, and "The Wizard of Oz," complete with a yellow brick road *(see FIGURE 2.8)*.

The workshop begins with an introduction describing the evening's activities. There should be a single main event, often a live performance by a scientist mixing, making, and concocting right there in front of the kids with clouds of smoke and much bravado. The remainder of the evening allows the audience to break into groups based on age and interest. There are usually one or two grade-level-appropriate films which reinforce a discussion of the scientific method. There is also a group of scientists and teachers who will help students choose project ideas—usually the most difficult part of getting started—and a room for library materials where parents and students can skim various books available at the local library. Because the fun of science is in the doing, we also provide an area where students can perform some simple hands-on experiments.

Encourage the entire family to come to the workshop. Provide movies, activities, and supervision for preschool children in a separate location. Students who will be participating in the fair and their parents are then free to enjoy and explore for the entire evening. In this informal workshop, parents and students can stay as long as they like, and before leaving, every parent and student receives a copy of the *Science Fair Handbook* with the registration form *(APPENDIX A and FIGURE 2.15)*.

FIGURE 2.15 **SCIENCE FAIR REGISTRATION FORM**

PLEASE RETURN THIS FORM TO THE SCHOOL SECRETARY BY _____.

(Date)

1. **This registration is for (circle one)**

   Individual entry   Partner entry*

   *Only K–6 students may work with a partner.
   The project will be judged at the higher grade level of the two students.

2. **Student's Name** _____

3. **School** _____

4. **Grade** _____

5. **Teacher** _____

6. **Home Address** _____

7. **Home Phone** _____

8. **Complete only if working with a partner:**

   Partner's Name _____

   School _____

   Grade _____

   Teacher _____

   Home Address _____

   Home Phone Number _____

FIGURE 2.15   *continued*

9. **Title of Project** _____

_____

10. **Describe your project by giving the following information:**

What question does my project answer? _____

_____

_____

What will I measure? _____

_____

_____

What will I change? _____

_____

_____

What will I keep the same? _____

_____

_____

11. **I agree to assist my child with his/her science project.**

Parent or Guardian _____

PLEASE CHECK TO **BE SURE YOU HAVE ANSWERED ALL 11 QUESTIONS.**
IF YOU ARE WORKING WITH A PARTNER,
DID YOUR PARTNER COMPLETE HIS/HER REGISTRATION FORM?

EVENT 3: THE MAIN EVENT: THE FAIR

The importance of the careful organization and preparation of the preceding six months is now evident the last week before the fair. With school and community support, your fair can meet its goal of being exciting and educational without being a large time burden on a few individuals.

Before Friday's Check-In The facility set-up for the day of the fair is completed by 5:00 p.m. the afternoon before the fair. *(See APPENDIX B, Form 2.)* This includes posting signs to direct students, preparing room arrangements, and setting up tables for project check-in and for the project display areas.

In the week before the fair, the students' project reports are previewed, grouped by grade level, and assigned to judging teams. *(The method for previewing the project reports is covered in CHAPTER 4, Producing a Fair Science Fair.)* Two student identification labels are placed on each student's Science Fair Judging Sheet: one is placed on the top half of the sheet, which becomes the confidential property of the Science Fair Steering Committee, and a second label is placed near the bottom of the sheet on the portion that is returned to the students with the judges' comments.

During the same time, the Volunteer Coordinator prepares the final list of all volunteers *(including their phone numbers)* for the Friday project check-in and for the day of the fair. Copies of volunteer instructions *(see APPENDIX B)* and name tags for all volunteers are prepared for the Fair Coordinator to distribute to volunteers as they arrive.

Once the project summaries/reports are received, the Computer Specialist prepares the Participants' Booklet, listing the names of all the students in the fair and their projects, check-in lists, and identification labels. School district personnel then arrange and duplicate the booklet, readying it for distribution on the day of the fair.

Friday's Check-In The Set-up and Supply Coordinator arranges the project check-in area with one table for each grade level. *(see APPENDIX B, Form 3.)* Volunteers are assigned to each table to greet students and check off their names on the list of participants.

(See APPENDIX B, Form 4.) Students are given a student identification label for their project. Parents are asked to indicate any special needs for judging times. They are given a list of volunteers whom they can call the next morning to find out the student's assigned judging time. (See FIGURE 2.16.) Students are then directed to the project display areas for project set-up. Volunteers are also available in the project display area to answer questions and assist students with setting up their projects.

By 7:00 p.m., project set-up is complete, and the Steering Committee begins preparing the final materials for the day of the fair. These activities are essential to the smooth running of the science fair (see APPENDIX B, Form 5).

FIGURE 2.16	**JUDGING TIME INQUIRIES**

ATTENTION ALL PARENTS AND JUNIOR SCIENTISTS:

As you know, the judging will begin at 9:15 a.m. If, however, you would like to know exactly what time your project is to be judged, then please call one of the phone numbers listed below between 7:45 and 8:45 a.m. tomorrow morning, March XX. *PLEASE BE CONSIDERATE AND OBSERVE THE TIME LIMITS. DO NOT CALL BEFORE 7:45 a.m.* Please arrive 15-20 minutes before the assigned time.

Names and phone numbers of volunteers are as follows:

Using parent requests for judging times, the committee can assign judging times for the students. This is done by placing an identification label on the Judging Tally Sheets (FIGURE 4.7) in the order that the projects will be judged. Judging times are assigned with twelve minutes allowed for K–3 projects, and fifteen minutes for grades 4–8 projects. Volunteers copy these tally sheets and post them outside the project display area, outside the Participants' Activities Room, and at the student check-in area. (NOTE: Projects are checked in on Friday evening but student check-in occurs Saturday morning when students arrive for the fair.) Copies are placed on the judging team's clipboard along with the project summaries/reports. Volunteers also prepare copies for the student escort volunteers and Steering Committee members, and later that evening they deliver copies to the parent volunteers who will receive telephone calls in the morning to confirm judging times. The originals stay in the Judges' Room for use later in the day, during score analysis.

On this night before the fair, the Committee may have to adjust the number of judges needed once they have a final project count, although almost all students who turn in project summaries/reports participate in the fair. Because it is possible that judges may cancel their commitment to the science fair at the last minute, it is advisable to have one or two alternates available.

Judges may preview projects from 7:00 p.m. to 9:00 p.m., while the Committee is making final preparations for the fair. This early project reviewing allows judges leisure time to see as many projects as they would like before the morning of the fair. Judges can read project summaries/reports at this time—a practice that allows more time in the morning and helps keep judging on schedule.

In addition to completing the Judging Tally Sheets, the Committee organizes the Judging Sheets *(two per project)* with each

FIGURE 2.17	TIME LINE OF EVENTS FOR THE DAY OF THE FAIR	
TIME	ACTIVITY	FIGURES
7:00 a.m.	Doors open	
7:00 a.m. – 8:20 a.m.	Judges arrive and preview projects (optional)	
8:15 a.m. – 8:30 a.m.	Judges' Workshop	Figure 4.3
8:30 a.m. – 8:50 a.m.	Parent volunteers arrive	Appendix B, Forms 7, 8, 9, & 10
8:50 a.m. – 9:15 a.m.	All Judges review papers and preview projects	
9:15 a.m. –11:00 a.m.	Primary grades judging, Students check in upon arrival	
9:15 a.m. –11:30 a.m.	Grades 4–8 judging	
11:00 a.m. –12:00 noon	Judging teams meet and discuss scores	Figures 4.4, 4.5, and 4.6
11:30 a.m. –1:45 p.m.	Scores checked and computer analyzed	
1:30 p.m. – 2:30 p.m.	Fair open to public	
1:30 p.m. – 3:00 p.m.	Award assignment and distribution	Appendix B, Form 11
3:00 p.m. – 3:20 p.m.	Award Ceremony	
3:20 p.m. – 3:30 p.m.	Clean-up	Appendix B, Form 12

of the clipboards with one judging sheet. *(Judges share the reports with the other member of their judging team in the morning.)* The other judge receives only a copy of the judging sheet. Each clipboard is prepared with a judge's name tag, which also bears the judging team identification number. The judging team is identified by student grade and team letter *(for example, three first-grade teams are designated 1A, 1B, and 1C).* The clipboards are organized by grade and by judging team in preparation for Saturday morning.

The Day of the Fair Committee members assist on the day of the fair whenever possible. Some members will come early in the day and make sure that coffee and refreshments are available for the judges.

Others will help with scoring and award distribution, while still others will help with clean-up at the end of the day. Parents are asked to donate baked goods for the judges, and many arrive Friday night during project set-up. A detailed time line of events for the day of the fair appears in *FIGURE 2.17.*

At 8:30 a.m., the Judges' Workshop begins *(see FIGURE 4.3).* This is an opportunity for the Fair Coordinator and Computer Specialist to review important points regarding judging and to answer any questions judges might have. Judging begins promptly at 9:15 a.m. From 8:50 to 9:15 a.m., judges can finish reading the project summaries/reports or can preview projects in their assigned grade level.

Students begin arriving at 9:00 a.m. and are checked in by volunteers stationed at the main entrance to the Participants' Activities Room *(see APPENDIX B, Forms 7 & 8).* Students are given a student identification label to wear as a name tag. This is especially important for younger students who may not hear their names called for judging. Volunteers are also present at the information table greeting other volunteers, handing out their name tags and answering questions for participants and their parents *(see APPENDIX B, Form 9)*.

Beginning at 9:15 a.m., students are escorted in small groups to the project display areas so that they are available whenever the judges are ready *(see APPENDIX B, Form 10)*. When their judging is complete, students return to the Participants' Activities Room. Students are in the project display area while they are being judged; otherwise they are involved in a variety of interesting activities in the Participants' Activities Room *(see APPENDIX B, Form 8)*. The project display area atmosphere remains quiet and calm and allows the judges a pleasant opportunity to interview the students. The quiet of the project display areas during judging is an important part of the fair organization, and it is possible because of the Participants' Activities Room.

The judging concludes by noon when the process of checking judges' scores begins. Students and parents leave the building at this time, but return later for public viewing and awards. As judging teams complete their scoring, they return their clipboards to the Judges' Room. It is a good idea to ask the teacher volunteers to check scores for addition errors and review judges' comments. We strongly encourage the judges to keep their comments positive and supportive with constructive criticism. This is not always easy to do and, as explained in *CHAPTER 4*, teacher volunteers review the comments and make minor wording changes, if necessary, to keep the tone positive. The judging team's scores are averaged at this time and entered on the original Judging Tally Sheets as Raw Scores. As each team member's scores are completed, they are sent to the Computer Room, where they are entered in the computer program FAIR, developed specifically for this purpose. The program is on the floppy disk available with this book, and instructions for its use are in *CHAPTER 4*, Producing a *Fair* Science Fair.

Awards assignment is done with the guidance of FAIR. This task is completed by 2:15 p.m. so that awards can be distributed at the project displays during community viewing. Even while score analysis is taking place, the fair is opened to the public at 1:30 p.m. Students are encouraged to return to the fair at this time and stand beside their project so they can answer questions for visitors. All students receive a first-, second-, or third-place ribbon and recognition on the stage at the Awards Ceremony at 3:00 p.m. *(Remember to have two awards available for projects done by partners and to call both partners' names when presenting awards.)* Outstanding awards are announced at the very end of the ceremony. This procedure keeps the audience waiting for all the awards to be given before leaving. The Fair Coordinator sends a copy of the awards list, along with pictures, to the local newspapers for publication.

Students must remove all projects from the display areas by 3:30 p.m. *(see APPENDIX B, Form 12).* Principals should encourage students to bring their projects to their school for display in the library or learning center.

EVENT 4: EVALUATION

Evaluating the fair once it is over is as important as all the planning that has gone on in the months preceding the fair. Producing a successful science fair is an ongoing process. Evaluation forms are invaluable to ensure continuous improvement and are given to parents, students, volunteers, committee members, teachers, and judges on the day of the fair.

Encourage all attendees to fill out an evaluation of your fair. It is important to see if there is a consensus for changes as well as to be in touch with the parents to determine what areas they feel need improvement. There is always something the Steering Committee can learn from the fair. Each evaluation gives you an opportunity to assess your strengths and identify your weaknesses. You must be sure that both the students and their parents enjoyed the entire process of the fair. It is important to be sure that the rules are definitive but light, and that the tone of all communication is always positive. Parents should know who to contact with a problem and should be given a prompt response whenever possible. The day of the fair is the best time to ask for feedback, so copies of evaluation forms are distributed in each Participants' Booklet and collected by the Steering Committee Members after the Awards Ceremony. A sample Evaluation Form appears in *FIGURE 2.11.*

An informal evaluation session takes place immediately after the fair. Steering Committee members who are present will meet when the scoring is complete to review areas for improvement that have arisen during the day—everything from parking problems to judging difficulties. The Committee is especially sensitive to the judges and their ability to relate to children. Judges who may be too severe for elementary students should not be asked to return the next year. However, at no time should the Committee change a judge's score. This is very important, as students are told repeatedly that the judges' decisions are final.

The Steering Committee meets about one month later to evaluate the fair, the logistics of check-in, the quality of the projects, and the day itself. By consensus, appropriate suggestions are integrated into next year's task time line after the evaluations from the science fair have been reviewed.

3

We first survey the plot,

then draw the model.

Shakespeare, *King Henry IV*,

Act 1, Sc. 3

SCIENCE EXPERIMENTS

A HOW-TO GUIDE

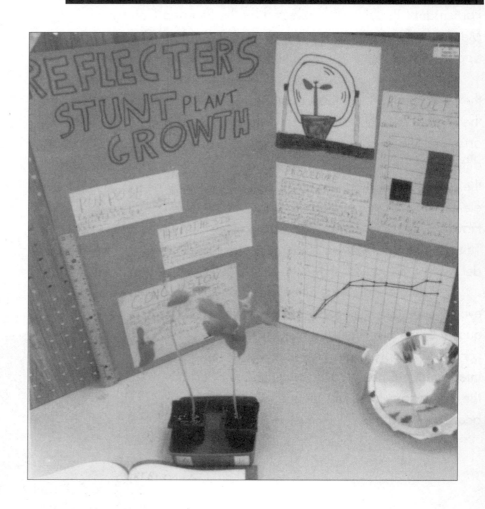

■ *What is an experiment? How is it different from a demonstration, invention, or survey? The term* experiment, *as used throughout this book, is the test of an object or theory in which one thing is changed while keeping everything else the same; a measurement is made of what happens as a result. In contrast, a demonstration is a display or model of a scientific principle or of how something works. (For example: How does a battery work?) An invention involves the design of a new system or equipment which might solve a problem or accomplish a task. (For example: A device which will tie someone's shoes.) A scientific survey is a comprehensive way of organizing*

information or material. (For example: A survey could be made of seashells found on the Atlantic Coast of North America.)

Only experiments involve a rather standard step-by-step procedure known as a scientific method. Because all student projects at our science fair are experiments, this chapter presents an explanation of a scientific method. We also include suggestions that help ensure that the measurements and results of experiments are correct. The same results should recur if someone else performed a similar experiment. (Doing a few standard things to ensure correctness is an important part of a science experiment.) Finally, we have developed a list of project titles in APPENDIX C, Project Ideas, which describe experiments suitable for grade-school students. These titles can be used directly for science fair projects or can lead to new ideas.

Because this chapter deals with science experiments in particular, while the remainder of the book is about science fairs in general, the information that follows is intended to be used differently from the other chapters. We intend this chapter to be used by parents and students together who will be selecting, doing, understanding, and presenting a science fair experiment. This information will also be helpful to teachers as it is designed to be a simple explanation of a scientific process of analysis. Suggestions and examples given can be modified for use with students at most elementary grade levels.

Keep in mind that younger students—particularly those in the primary grades (K–2)—will need more help than older students. Whether the help comes from a parent, other family member, neighbor, or teacher, the assistance and guidance should be only what the student needs. This will vary depending upon not only the age, but also the ability level of the student. As parents reflect upon the abilities of their children, it will become fairly obvious what degree of guidance and assistance each child will need. For example, a parent may need to guide a first-grader through his or her project in the order we suggest and even pose pertinent questions along the way. The parent will certainly have to write or type the child's project summary. What is important to remember, however, is to let the first-grader do the thinking and doing.

PREPARING A PROJECT

Preparing a project for a science fair consists of:

1. Selecting a topic and an idea of how to do the experiment *(no details are needed yet)*;
2. Planning and building the experiment;
3. Performing the experiment, taking measurements, and thinking about what happened; and
4. Preparing materials for the science fair that briefly explain the idea of the project, what was done, and what happened. These items are used in:
   a. the display of the project,
   b. a brief written report about the project, and
   c. a brief talk about the project.

The first step of selecting a topic is part of a standard method for looking into a problem or performing an experiment—*a scientific method.* Such a method consists of several steps in an order that produces a clear experiment. Also, there are standard things to do or check at some steps that help with the correctness of the results. Being correct about what was measured and what caused things to change is a very important aspect of investigations in science. In some cases, important consequences are at stake. If, for example, based on experimental results a new device is designed and built to be placed in every new car, it is very important that the results occur over and over again in the same way. If they don't, a lot of money and perhaps personal safety would be at stake. Thus, it is important that some things be done during certain steps of the experiment to help ensure correctness.

The number of steps in a scientific method and the exact content of each varies according to the scientist using the method and the branch of science involved. However, the basic order of the steps and their general content are rather standard. *FIGURE 3.1* lists the steps of a scientific method that can be applied to science fair experiments.

SCIENTIFIC METHOD

FIGURE 3.1	**STEPS IN A SCIENTIFIC METHOD**

STEP #1 **Select a question to be answered by the experiment.**
STEP #2 **Form a hypothesis.**
STEP #3 **Perform the experiment.**
STEP #4 **Prepare the results**.
STEP #5 **Explain the results.**
STEP #6 **Draw the conclusions.**

STEP 1: SELECTING A QUESTION TO BE ANSWERED BY THE EXPERIMENT

This question must be one that can be answered by a student who should be able to do the experiment. Students must be able to understand the subject and do most of the work. The question should not be answered by a simple *yes* or *no*. For example, "How does salt affect the freezing point of water?" is a better question than, "Does salt affect the freezing point of water?" We already know from everyday life that adding salt to water will lower the freezing point–that is why we put salt on icy roads. But an experiment can determine how much the freezing point changes depending on the amount or type of salt added.

In order to write a project question, the student must first select a project topic. It is helpful to begin by making a list of science areas that are interesting to the student. These may be areas that are studied in school or seen at a museum, in the movies, or on television. Perhaps the student is wondering about something that he or she has read or heard or noticed elsewhere.

It is a good idea to encourage the students to talk to parents, teachers, and scientists about their ideas. It is also helpful to take a list of ideas to the library and see what information can be found. The many books written on science fair projects are sure to be helpful in learning more about possible topics. The student should be alert for interesting ideas or different ways to make measurements or construct equipment. Items that are a bit out of the ordinary make especially interesting projects.

A Word of Caution

 Most books on science fair projects do not differentiate between experiments and demonstrations, surveys, or inventions. Because in our science fair projects should be experiments, students may need help selecting questions that can be answered through an experiment or that can easily be made into one.

Variables To differentiate an experiment from a demonstration, we have identified two key elements of an experiment: the variables and the measurements. All experiments must contain at least these two important elements.

All things that can or will change in an experiment are called *variables.* Variables can be divided into three groups:

1. A *manipulated variable* is one that is changed on purpose in the experiment. It is one of the two elements a science fair project must have to be called an experiment *(unlike a demonstration, survey, or invention).* How interesting the project will be often depends on what manipulated variable is chosen.

2. The *responding variable* changes because of the alteration made to the manipulated variable. This change in the responding variable is one that can be measured, and it is this measurement that leads to the results of the experiment and eventually to an answer to the experimental question.

3. *Controlled variables* are all of the other conditions that one attempts to keep the same while the manipulated variable is changed. If more than one variable changes at a time, it is usually not possible to tell which change caused the result. Controlled variables will be referred to simply as controls throughout the remainder of this book.

Measurements In an experiment, it is best if there is only one manipulated and one responding variable. A measurement *(of the responding variable)* must be made to tell what effect a change in the manipulated variable has on the responding variable. A measurement is the second of the two things that a project must have to be called an experiment *(as opposed to a demonstration, survey, or invention).*

Depending on his or her age, the student may need help in arriving at the best way to make the most accurate measurements. The accuracy required from the measuring device depends on the particular experiment. For example, if time is to be measured between two events, should a clock that measures hours, minutes, and seconds be used, or is the measurement of hours and minutes accurate enough? The answer depends on the time difference between the events.

The best measurements are those that are objective: time, temperature, weight, length, and so on. Subjective measurements, like some visual observations or taste, cloud the results of an experiment. For example, mold growth experiments are popular at science fairs, but generally the only practical way to measure differences in the amount of growth is by visual inspection, perhaps accompanied by photographs and drawings. If the difference in the amount of growth between two specimens of mold on bread is small, two people observing them could easily have different opinions as to which is the larger amount, and so could the science fair judges. Although at our fair we have chosen to accept subjective measurements such as visual inspections, they are usually not good measurements and certainly not acceptable if other objective measurements can, in fact, be made.

Turning a Demonstration into an Experiment A demonstration is something built or done to show that an event happens or to explain some scientific principle. It lacks some things that would make it an experiment. A student might find a demonstration topic that is very interesting to him or her so it is helpful to be able to turn the question into an experiment.

A demonstration is usually missing a variable, a measurement, or both. By adding these two key elements and following the scientific method, a demonstration can often be made into an experiment. For example, a student may have wondered about how much water flows in the pipes in his or her house during a shower or through a garden hose. The question might be asked, "How much water flows through a garden hose?" Doing the project might consist of attaching a hose to a basement sink or outside faucet and measuring the amount of water that flows into a container in one minute. Although the project is one that is in an interesting area of science, and even though the rate of water flow *(amount of water that flows per minute)* is not something that many people know, this project would be classified as a demonstration. The amount of water that flows in one minute *(or the flow rate)* is something that can be demonstrated. The student may have understood that the number of gallons of water that flows depends on the principle of friction between the water and the hose, but an experiment was not performed and the whole scientific reasoning and discovery process was not used. There was a measurement for the project–the number of gallons of water collected–but there is no variable in this demonstration project. Therefore, an experiment was not performed according to our basic criteria for the science fair.

The project could be made into an experiment simply by adding a variable. For example, the student might choose to change the length of the hose and again measure the amount of water that flows in one minute. The length of hose becomes the manipulated variable and the amount of water the responding variable. The controls *(controlled variables)* are such items as diameter of hose, temperature of water, the opening of the faucet valve, absence of kinks or bends in the hose, and so on.

Be Creative in Selecting a Topic Creativity is an important element of any science experiment. Scientists and engineers are constantly in search of new and better ways to solve problems. New approaches often lead to new information and understanding. Students should be encouraged to give consideration to topics that are just a bit different from popular topics. A slight variation from a popular topic in the form of the variable chosen, the equipment used or the measurement taken can add interest to the project. It also adds interest to ask a question where the answer is not well known. However, popular topics should not be completely discounted. A popular topic, one that is frequently chosen for science fair projects, is often brand new to students. Such topics can make fine science fair projects if they are done well according to the scientific method. For example, experiments using plants and light, fertizilations, or

watering solutions are commonly used for science fairs. However, the rate of watering is not usually selected and yet could present an interesting alternative to a rather common topic. Such a question might be asked: How does rate of watering affect plant growth? To answer this question, a student could do an experiment watering some plants with 1 cup of water on the first day of each week and watering other plants with 1/7 of a cup each day for seven days. With proper controls and careful use of all of the steps of the scientific method, a student could turn this common topic into an interesting experiment.

Whichever type of topic the student chooses, he or she should read some background material to get a rough idea of how he or she might do the experiment. The student should think about what equipment will be needed, the variable to be manipulated, the things to be kept constant *(controls),* and the measurements to be made.

At this point, the student has enough information to write the experiment question. Changes can be made up until the final days before the science fair. In the garden hose flow example, a student might decide that he or she is interested in the flow of water. The idea of experimenting with flow leads to the topic of garden hoses. The student may narrow the focus for the experiment further after reading that there is quite a lot of friction between a flowing fluid and a long pipe or hose, and friction reduces flow. This is similar to how the slight friction between a sled and snow slows down the sled. The student might then choose the length of the hose as the manipulated variable and the question might be, "How is the amount of water that flows in a garden hose affected by the length of the hose?" Thinking and talking about the experiment, the student might find other variables that are even more interesting. For example, thinking that bends or coils in the hose also add friction, a student might coil a single hose and measure the flow for different shapes and sizes of the coil. The hose could be formed into a square with rounded corners to test the effect of tight bends on the flow.

In this example, the science area of fluid flow and the variable of hose length are not often chosen for science fair experiments, and they both make the project more interesting. The question implies that length affects the flow of water and the experiment asks how much is the effect. The answer (results) should be in terms of measured differences of the amount of water flow through different length hoses. The details of the experiment are yet to be determined, but this question would provide a good start and a clearly focused topic. The student would know the question to be answered, have an idea about both the equipment needed and how the experiment could be done. He or she would even know the measurement to be made and the manipulated variable to be tested.

STEP 2: FORMING A HYPOTHESIS

Based on the student's background reading and personal experiences, the student should have an idea about at least part of the answer to his or her question. That idea is called the *hypothesis (or best guess)*. The hypothesis gives the student a general guide as to what to expect from the experiment.

In choosing the garden hose flow experiment, a student might think that longer hoses produce more friction than shorter hoses. The hypothesis would be that the amount of water that flows in a period of time is expected to be less for longer hoses. Or the student might have noticed from watering a lawn or garden that the water spray is not as strong for longer hoses. This fact might lead him or her to make the same hypothesis.

The hypothesis need not be very detailed. According to the hypothesis in the flow example, the amount of flow will decrease for longer hoses, but it does not attempt to say by how much. If the hose is made twice as long, will the amount of flow be half as much? If the student knew this answer, there would be no need to do the experiment. The hypothesis does not have to answer all of the details of the question. In fact, the hypothesis does not even have to be correct. Proof of the hypothesis will come by doing the experiment. Two examples of the process to this point are summarized in *FIGURE 3.2*. The experiment question, hypothesis, and variables are listed for the hose experiment and for an experiment involving the placement of weights on a toy car *(Captain Planet® Geo-cruiser)*.

FIGURE 3.2	BEGINNINGS OF EXPERIMENTS		
QUESTION	HYPOTHESIS	VARIABLES	CONTROLS
Which position of the weight makes the Geo-cruiser go farthest?	The weight in the middle will make the Geo-cruiser go farthest.	*Manipulated:* The position of the weight—front, middle, back	The ramp, Geo-cruiser, starting position
		Responding: How far the Geo-cruiser travels	
How does hose length affect the amount of water that flows?	The longer the hose the smaller the amount of water that will flow through it.	*Manipulated:* The length of the hose	Diameter of hoses, Water pressure, Temperature, Opening of faucet valve, Bends or kinks in hoses
		Responding: The amount (gallons) of water that flows through the hose in 1 minute	

STEP 3: PERFORMING THE EXPERIMENT

This step of the scientific method has several parts. The details of the experiment are planned, materials are collected, and equipment is assembled or constructed. Tests are done, and checks are made about the correctness of measurements. As the experiment is performed, changes from the plans may be made to make a better experiment. After this step, the results will be grouped and studied. Finally, conclusions will be made.

Variables There are many parts of the experiment to plan. The manipulated and responding variables must be chosen, and all controls needed to assure that nothing else changes must be identified. In the garden hose experiment, the manipulated variable is the length of hose, and the responding variable is the amount of water that flows in a fixed period of time. Other variables that could change during the experiment should be considered and controls decided to keep them constant. It is important to choose the range of the manipulated variable so that a measurable change will occur in the responding variable. If there is no change, the experiment results are usually not too interesting.

Experiments with consumer products are somewhat different in experimental design. For example, if the student is testing the strength of various paper towels, the manipulated variable is the brand of paper towel and everything else is controlled: the size of the sheet tested, the amount of water used to wet the towel, the weight applied to the towel, and so on. In this example, creativity in the method for testing paper towel strength is a good way to add interest to the experiment.

Controls Controls are very important to the correctness of the measurements and the results. The student will want to be as sure as possible that the change in the responding variable is due only to changes that were made to the manipulated variable and not to other variable changes that were not controlled. The student should think of as many things as possible that might have an affect on the responding variable. The experiment should keep the important things all the same during each test to make sure that they are not affecting the results. In the garden hose flow experiment, anything else besides hose length that adds friction will also cause a change in flow. Kinks or bends in the hose as well as different diameters and materials change friction. Therefore, in all tests, these variables should be controlled: hoses are laid out straight without bends, all hoses are the same diameter, and all hoses are made of the same material.

Measurements Measurements, accuracy, and measuring devices have been discussed previously. These items are clearly key parts of an experiment, and they deserve some thought. In the garden hose example, there should be a clear difference in amounts measured between tests with different hose lengths. By doing some quick test in a sink with a bucket and watch, it was determined that the maximum flow expected is about four gallons in one minute. The availability of a five-gallon container, with marks every quarter gallon, made it a good choice for the measuring device: one minute was chosen for the time period. As long as the differences between tests with different hose lengths would measure more than one quarter gallon, this container would be adequate.

Equipment and Procedure The student should select the materials to be collected or built that will become the experiment equipment. Students should think of more than one way to make parts of the equipment and choose the ways that are simpler to use and easier to build. *(Many successful engineers, who design the things in the world around us, are well aware of the KISS principle—Keep It Simple, Students.)* With the needed equipment in mind, the student can plan how the tests will be done, in what order, how many, what will be recorded, how many times the same test will be repeated, and so on. By doing the easier tests first, the student can get used to the equipment. These first tests might be gentler on the equipment, shorter, and so on. It may be better to change some things after these first tests. It is important to keep thinking and evaluating throughout the experiment. The student should have photographs of the experiment in progress for use later in the science fair display.

Repetition Repeating tests several times each is also very important to the correctness and quality of any measurements and results. Each time the same test is repeated, it is likely that the measurements will change somewhat. If the change is small each time, it is a good sign that everything in the experiment is controlled. The best value of the measurement is usually the average of the repeated tests. Younger students can pick the best representative number even if they cannot calculate the average. If the change in measurements is large each time the test is repeated, it usually means that something is changing in the experiment that the student did not expect. It is desirable to get rid of this change if possible. Averaging the measurements from these tests becomes even more important if they are used in the results. In the flow experiment, it is important that the water pressure remain the same during the tests. This pressure is probably something that may be difficult to control so all the tests might be done in one day or at the same time each day to reduce the chances that water pressure will change much during the tests.

Repeating tests also shows if something went wrong with one or more measurements. If a test is repeated six times, and in five the measurements are within two seconds of each other, but in the sixth the measurement is different by ten seconds, the student might suspect that something was different about that test or a mistake was made. The student might redo these tests or simply discard the one measurement that was very different, especially if the other tests did not show such a difference in repeated measurements.

In the garden hose flow example, the student may have borrowed four hoses each 100 feet long from neighbors. The hoses should be made of the same material and have the same diameter. The plan for the tests would be to attach one hose to the faucet and measure the amount of water that flows into the container in a period of one minute. Then two hoses would be attached together and the measurement repeated, and so on, with three, four, and no hoses. The amount of water, the time of day, and any comments about the test would be recorded in each case. The student may have made the decision to repeat each test five times, and might change this number later depending on how close together the measurements turn out to be.

Assembling the Equipment Having planned for the equipment, the way the test will be run, and the measurements that will be made, it is time for the student to build the equipment and make up pages where measurements and comments will be written during the experiment, the data sheets. A sample data sheet for the hose experiment is shown in *FIGURE 3.3*. Here, measurements of water in the container are being made to the nearest quarter gallon as indicated. Tests are to be made for each hose length, and repeat tests are listed, too. Anything different about a test should be noted in the comments area provided. Many books on science fair projects provide additional discussion of data sheets.

FIGURE 3.3		SAMPLE DATA SHEET FOR HOSE EXPERIMENT		
DATE	TIME	LENGTH OF HOSE (Feet)	AMOUNT OF WATER (Gallons)	COMMENTS
3/1	4:15 p.m	0	4	Water was run 5 min before test
3/1	4:30 p.m.	100	2 1/4	
		200	1 1/2	Water flowed through hose 2 min at start
		300	1 1/4	
		400	1	
		0	4	
		0	4 1/4	
		0	4	
		0	4	
		100	2 1/4...	
...	...	...	...	...
...	...	...	...	...
...	...	...	...	...
3/5	4:40 p.m.	400	1	Slight surge occurred during test

As the experiment is built, plans may need to be modified. It is important to control all things that might affect the responding variable. In the garden hose flow example, the idea of using hose as long as 400 feet is good because it is likely to show a large measurable change in flow. However, laying that length of hose out straight is not practical in a basement and perhaps not even outside depending on the location of the faucet, buildings, and streets. This might mean that the control needs to be modified to lay out the hose with only very gradual bends around a basement room and to keep the same bends for all hoses.

Performing the Tests Now everything is ready. All of the tests are planned, the equipment is built, and all that has to be done is to turn on the water. A prominent engineer, who often performed research experiments, once said that after months of careful planning, and writing down the details of every test to be done, she only committed to doing the first test on the list. She meant that she probably was not able to think of everything in advance and that she might need to make changes after running some tests.

The same is often true of science fair experiments. The student should start by following his or her plan, and make changes as needed. It may be necessary to start the tests all over again after making some changes, so students are encouraged to start early. The student should start the first test according to plan. Measurements should be taken and written on the data sheets. Notes *(comments)* should be made as to what happened during the test. If everything goes well, the student can go on to the next test. A problem with equipment or procedure may occur during the first test or may not occur until the manipulated variable gets very large or very small. Of course, there may be no problems at all. Performing the easier tests first will help the student see how the equipment works, and it will be easier to find the cause of any problems that occur.

In the example of the garden hose flow, an equipment

problem might have occurred using the five-gallon container to measure the amount of water. The container available was a washtub with a large diameter, resulting in the quarter-gallon marks being close together. It was difficult to read the water level between marks, so a tall container was found with a smaller diameter and more space between the quarter-gallon marks. Changing the container is acceptable *(after a few tests revealed the problem),* but all tests should be done with the new, more accurate container.

A problem with the procedure might also arise with the garden hose experiment. A reasonable test procedure might have been to attach one end of a hose to the faucet, put the free end into the container, and turn on the water. But after doing this once or twice, the student might notice that when the water is first turned on, it takes some time before the flow becomes steady; the amount of time varies for different length hoses. A better procedure would be to first start the flow into another container or onto the ground until it becomes steady and then move the hose to the container and start timing. If this procedure was thought of in advance—fine. If not, it could be changed after a few tests were run, and there would not be much loss of time or effort. When all the tests are finished, it is time to try to understand what happened.

STEP 4: PREPARING THE RESULTS

In this step, the measurements are reviewed and organized to show what happened in the experiment. Usually, tables, graphs, and charts are made to show the measurements in different ways. Sometimes, however, the measurements themselves are not used but rather something is determined from them. In the garden hose experiment, graphs of gallons of water versus hose length might be made. For older students who understand the mathematics, flow rate *(gallons per minute)* may be substituted for gallons. The flow rate is the number of gallons collected divided by the measured time in minutes.

$$\textit{Flow rate} = \frac{\textit{Number of gallons of water collected}}{\textit{Number of minutes of flow}}$$

Since the time was one minute in every test, the calculation of flow rate is not difficult. The units of gallons per minute *(gpm)* is a standard that many people understand. The number of gallons measured in the experiment and the flow rate behave in the same

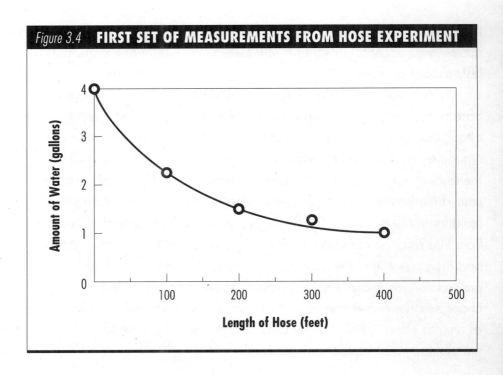

Figure 3.4   **FIRST SET OF MEASUREMENTS FROM HOSE EXPERIMENT**

way; they both decrease as the hose gets longer. Different types of charts may be used *(such as line graphs, bar graphs, or pie charts)*. Use the ones that seem to show the results most clearly. In the garden hose example, a line graph or a bar graph would be good choices to show how much the flow decreased as the hose got longer. A sample is shown in *FIGURE 3.4* for the five lengths of water hoses: 0, 100, 200, 300, and 400 ft. The circles represent the measurements, and the line through them shows the trend *(direction of change)*. If most of the measurements are alike in a repeated group and one is different, the student should check any comments written at the time of the test in question to see if the cause can be determined. If something different happened during one test, it may not be a good idea to include that measurement with the others. For example, if someone turned on the shower while tests were being done with one of the garden hose lengths, the water pressure could have been very different in that test from all of the others. That one test measurement should be discarded since all variables were not closely controlled. However, it is not acceptable in the scientific method to discard measurements without a good reason. The one test that is different may, in fact, be due to something very real which might be lost by discarding that measurement.

It is helpful to make some of these charts as tests are being done. The student might like to finish them with time to do a few more tests if needed to improve the results. For example, if the cause is not known as to why one measurement is quite different from a repeated group, the student could repeat the whole group of tests to show that the different measurement did not recur.

It is also possible that the charts *(or graphs)* might point to the need for more measurements that would make the results clearer. In the garden hose flow example, there are five flows to graph, one for each length of hose: 100 feet, 200 feet, 300 feet, 400 feet, and no hose at all. In looking at the graph, the student might notice that the biggest change happened between 0 and 100 feet of hose and that more points on the graph would make him or her more sure of the results. By adding a 50-foot length of hose to the end of each original length, five more measurements can be made doubling the number of points on the graph and adding one point where the flow change was largest. A graph of the results of all ten tests is shown in *FIGURE 3.5*. By making the graphs early, the student would have time before the science fair to add tests if they are needed.

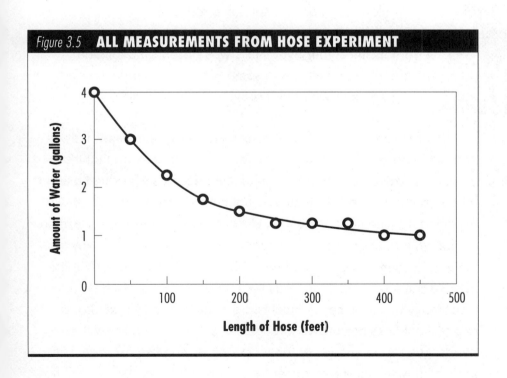

Figure 3.5   **ALL MEASUREMENTS FROM HOSE EXPERIMENT**

STEP 5: EXPLAINING THE RESULTS

Depending on the experiment, there will be more or less to think about in this step, but many students do not give enough time or thought to this important step in a scientific method. By now the measurements have been grouped and graphed in different ways to show *what* happened in the experiment. The student should try to understand *why* or *how* it happened. What caused the results? It is helpful to look at the graphs and try to find patterns. Students should ask questions like, "Do things keep getting larger or smaller, or do they get large and then small?" and "What are the likely causes of these trends in the results?" The student should use numbers whenever possible to describe changes.

The experiment is finished. It is time for the scientist to sit back, put up his or her feet, and think about what happened and how it all fits together. The following questions are worth taking some time to consider:

- What does this result mean?
- Are there other times or places when similar results would be expected to happen?
- Would it be important for some reason?
- Did the results turn out according to the hypothesis?
- If not, since your hypothesis was based on available information that was in some way similar to your experiment, why did it prove to be incorrect?

Sometimes the causes of results are clear; sometimes they're not. In the garden hose flow example, the charts showed that the amount of water that flowed in one minute decreased as the hose got longer, but doubling the length did not cut the amount in half. It was expected that the flow amount would decrease because there is more friction with a longer hose. The hypothesis was correct, but why was the flow amount not cut in half when the length was doubled? If the hose became twice as long, was the friction twice as much? Apparently not. The measurements are re-plotted in *FIGURE 3.6*, and two straight lines are drawn through the points to help show the trends. The results show that for shorter hose lengths *(less than 150 feet)* the flow change was rather large, while for long lengths the flow change was much smaller. These results show that if a short hose is being used, and say 50 feet of additional hose is added, the flow would be reduced considerably as shown by the straight line through the larger flow measurements. If a long hose is used, the flow is already low, and adding 50 more feet of hose does not affect it much. The students should use numbers from their charts to show what is meant by long, short, large, and small changes. Although these exact results may not apply to a hose of a different material or diameter, the generalization that the flow amount changes

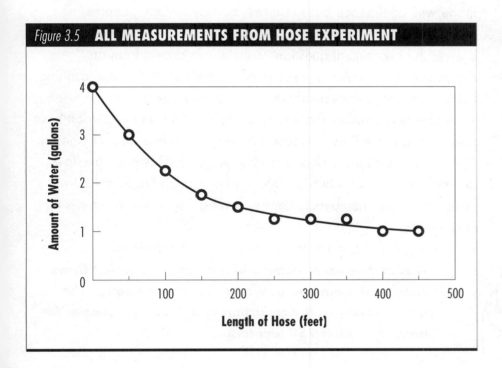

Figure 3.5 **ALL MEASUREMENTS FROM HOSE EXPERIMENT**

as a result of whether the hose is short or long applies to any hose or pipe.

There are usually interesting questions to think about that are related to the experiment and the results. Such things can be included in this step of the scientific method *(explaining the results)* as students are thinking about what the results mean. For example, here the student measured the amount of flow with no hose *(a hose of zero length)*. What about the other extreme, a very long hose? Based on the results of the experiment, what would happen if the hose got as long as 1000 feet or one mile? A judgment could be made based on the graph of flow amount versus hose length shown in *FIGURE 3.5*. The graph goes up to 450 feet of hose, and the student could continue the same shape of the line out to the longer lengths. This process is actually dangerous in science because the scientist cannot assume nothing new will happen as the hose length increases.

STEP 6: DRAWING CONCLUSIONS

The final step of any scientific method is to draw conclusions from what has happened. Conclusions, general statements that can be made with confidence based on results, may include patterns, measured values, changes, and so on. One of the conclusions should answer the experiment question. Conclusions drawn from an experiment are usually in the form of short statements. The reasoning behind the conclusions is drawn from the previous step as the experimenter considers the meaning of the results. In the garden hose flow example, the flow decreased by more than one quarter when a 50-foot hose was increased to a 100-foot hose. However, the flow decreased very little when a 50-foot hose was added to a 150-foot hose. Try to give numbers for answers when reporting experimental conclusions.

A general conclusion stated in terms of friction is:

Friction between water and the hose in which it flows reduces the amount of water that flows through the hose. However, the reduction effect is much greater for hoses less than 150 feet long.

The conclusions can be taken one step further by applying the results to a hose used to water lawns. How important is the length of a hose for watering a lawn with the type of hose tested? The results show that the answer is different for large and small lawns. There is a large benefit to keeping the hose length short and not having extra hose if the lawn is small. The flow rate will be much higher if a 50-foot hose is used instead of a 100-foot hose. For a large lawn, it does not make much difference if there is some extra hose. There will be very little flow rate difference between 150 and 200 feet of hose and even less between 200 and 250 feet. This last conclusion adds more interest to the student's work, and it shows that the student thought about the implications of the experiment's results in a real situation.

THE SCIENTIFIC METHOD AND PRIMARY STUDENTS: ERIC'S EXPERIMENT

We are often asked if it is possible to teach the scientific method to younger students. We have found that primary students are very capable of understanding the steps we have outlined. To illustrate this point, we have selected an experiment performed by a first-grade student from our district, Eric, at one of our recent fairs. This experiment was judged "Outstanding."

The experiment tested how the placement of a small weight in different positions on a toy vehicle affected how far the vehicle traveled. While the concept of weight and its effect on movement is not difficult, the careful execution of this experiment, with proper variables, measurements, and repeated trials, follows all the steps of our scientific method and is easily understandable by primary students.

STEP 1: SELECTING A QUESTION TO BE ANSWERED BY THE EXPERIMENT

Which position of the weight makes the Geo-cruiser go farthest? This is an interesting question, one that needs more than a simple "yes" or "no" answer and lends itself to an experimental solution. This question is not typically explored at science fairs and most people would not know how to answer it.

STEP 2: FORMING A HYPOTHESIS

This is the student's opportunity to predict the outcome of the experiment by both reading and discussing his or her ideas with teachers or parents. This will also help to determine the experimental design.

> *Eric's Hypothesis:* The weight placed in the middle will make the Geo-cruiser go the farthest.

STEP 3: PERFORMING THE EXPERIMENT

A young student will need some assistance in designing the experiment and selecting the variables and controls. For Eric's experiment, the manipulated variable *(the one thing that he changed)* was the placement of the weight: front, middle, or back. The responding variable, the factor that changed as a result of a change in the manipulated variable, was the distance traveled by the Geo-cruiser. The controls—those factors that kept constant—were the ramp and the starting position of the vehicle. *(By performing the experiment all at one time, Eric never moved the ramp position, so he did not have to consider variations in the floor surface which might have affected his results.)* Eric also performed one run of the experiment with no weight added to the car. This test gave him information on how the car would perform without adding any weight. This data could be compared to Eric's other tests to show how adding weight in different places on the car changed the distance the car traveled.

Once Eric selected variables and determined controls, he was ready to prepare any necessary test equipment and gather materials needed for the experiment.

Equipment and Materials:
>   small weight
>   Captain Planet ® Geo-cruiser
>   tape measure
>   ramp
>   tape
>   yardstick

The Steps of Eric's Experiment: The No-Weight Test

1.   Place the ramp in an open, level area on a hard-surfaced floor.
2.   Tape the tape measure to the floor to serve as a ready measuring device.
3.   Place the Geo-cruiser at the top of the ramp with the rear wheels hanging over the back of the ramp.
4.   Lift the rear wheels slightly to release the Geo-cruiser and allow it to move down the ramp.
5.   Measure the distance traveled by the Geo-cruiser.
6.   Repeat this test ten times and record the data.

Once Eric completed his no-weight test and made any necessary adjustments, he was ready to do to begin his experiment with weights.

The Experiment

1. Tape the weight to the top of the Geo-cruiser so that it is located at the front of the vehicle.
2. Repeat steps 1 through 6 above.

Eric followed this same procedure after he placed the weight on the back of the Geo-cruiser and in the middle. His data appears in the following table. An older student could average the results from the 10 trials and calculate the average distance for each test. However, a primary student might need some assistance. By graphing the results in order of smallest to largest measurement, a primary student could easily select the number in the middle that best represents the "average" distance that the car traveled. *(See FIGURES 3.8, 3.9, 3.10, and 3.11.)*

FIGURE 3.7	DISTANCE TRAVELED GEO-CRUISER IN INCHES		
NO-WEIGHT TEST	WEIGHT PLACED ON FRONT	WEIGHT PLACED ON BACK	WEIGHT PLACED IN MIDDLE
105	105 1/2	110	122
105	97 1/2	109 1/2	120 1/2
105	98 1/2	107 1/2	119 1/4
103 1/2	97 1/2	106	120
104	98	110	114 1/2
103	99 1/2	109	109
104	97 1/2	106 1/2	106 1/2
104	98	106 1/2	107 1/2
103 1/2	98 1/2	107	105 1/2
105	94 1/2	108 1/2	108 1/2
Avg. 104 1/4	Avg. 98 1/2	Avg. 108 1/2	Avg. 113 1/2

STEP 4: PREPARING THE RESULTS

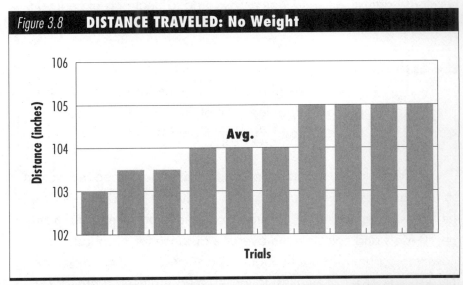

Figure 3.8 — **DISTANCE TRAVELED: No Weight**

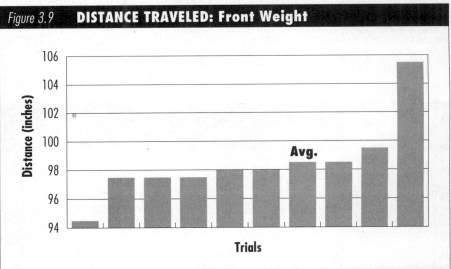

Figure 3.9 — **DISTANCE TRAVELED: Front Weight**

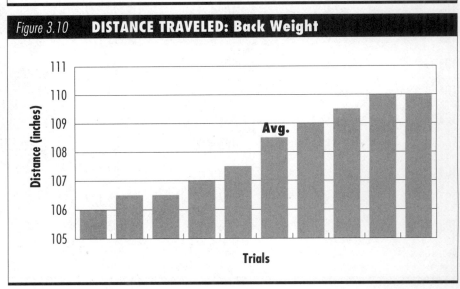

Figure 3.10 — **DISTANCE TRAVELED: Back Weight**

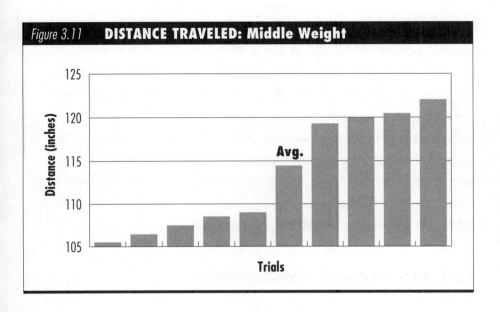

Figure 3.11 **DISTANCE TRAVELED: Middle Weight**

STEP 5: EXPLAINING THE RESULTS

Eric found that the weight placed in the middle of the Geo-cruiser made it go the farthest, even farther *(9 1/4" farther)* than with no weight at all. While his hypothesis—placing the weight in the middle of the car would make it go the farthest—was in fact, true, it was not easy for him to explain why the weight placed in the back and the middle actually improved the distance the Geo-cruiser traveled *(by 4" and 9 1/4" respectively)*, while the weight placed on the front made the vehicle go a shorter distance, compared to no weight at all. All of these results are shown in *FIGURE 3.12*.

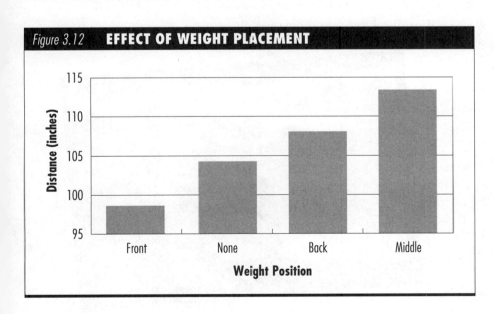

Figure 3.12 **EFFECT OF WEIGHT PLACEMENT**

Eric read some primary books on friction and discussed his results with his parents. He decided that putting the weight in front must increase the friction between the Geo-cruiser's front wheels and the ramp and so the vehicle actually goes a shorter distance. However, the Geo-cruiser is made of plastic, which is a rather light material, and it actually travels farther with some additional weight. Eric thought that perhaps the weight placed in the back presses down too hard on the rear wheels, increasing the friction between the rear wheels and the ramp, and keeping the Geo-cruiser from going as far as it does when the weight is in the middle.

STEP 6: DRAWING CONCLUSIONS

Eric thought about cars and decided that his car travels farthest if most of the weight is in the middle, and next farthest if most of the weight is in the back. The worst place for the weight is in the front. Compared to no weight, the middle-weighted car went 9 1/4" farther, the back-weighted car went 4" farther, and the front-weighted car stopped 5 3/4" short. It seemed from Eric's experiment that having the engine in the front of real cars is the worst place to put it. From his experiment, Eric thought that people should try cars with engines in the middle.

This connection between experimental results and the real world is very important to the student's understanding of the experiment. Thinking about the experiment and the principles behind it is the student's opportunity to project what the experiment might mean if applied to other things.

THE DAY OF THE SCIENCE FAIR

The experiment is complete, and it is now time to prepare the project for the science fair. The student must now tell others all about his or her experiment. The student may have done an excellent job with the experiment, but if he or she does not communicate well, nobody will ever know.

Communication about the project is done in three ways:
- The display of the project that will be seen by the judges, parents, teachers, students, and interested members of the community;
- A brief written report that will be read by the judges; and
- A brief talk to be given to the judges.

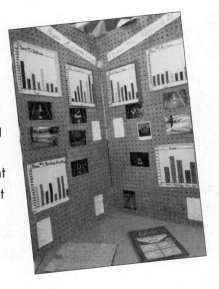

A good approach in all cases is to explain the experiment according to the steps of the scientific method that were followed in performing it. In each case, the student should "tell a story" about the experiment starting with the question and hypothesis, followed by the experiment with its measurements, variables, equipment and procedures, and ending with the results and conclusions. The key is to include all the important things clearly and concisely.

PROJECT DISPLAY

Each project must have a visual display to be used at the science fair. Actual equipment used in the project can be included in the display if there is room in the area provided to the student. It is most likely that there won't be room for everything, so the student will have to decide what are the most important things to show about the experiment. At our science fair, each project is allotted a space 30 inches deep by 36 inches wide. We impose a height restriction of 5 feet for safety reasons. A three-part board works well. It can be constructed of a center board and two wings arranged in a U-shape. Posterboard may be used if it is reinforced so that it stands on the table without much sagging.

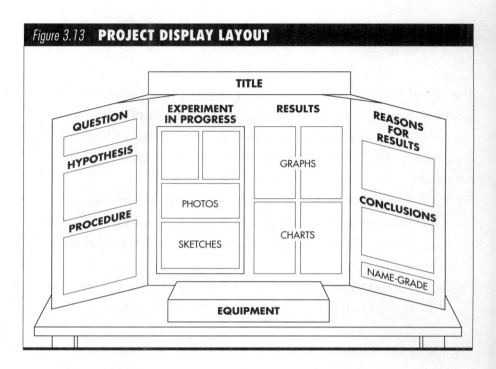

Figure 3.13 **PROJECT DISPLAY LAYOUT**

TITLE

QUESTION

HYPOTHESIS

PROCEDURE

EXPERIMENT IN PROGRESS

PHOTOS

SKETCHES

RESULTS

GRAPHS

CHARTS

REASONS FOR RESULTS

CONCLUSIONS

NAME-GRADE

EQUIPMENT

The display is similar to both the written and oral summaries that are prepared. It should follow the steps of the experiment and tell the same story. The display is a way to tell many people at one time about the experiment. They should be able to tell the most important things from the display without even talking with the student.

One suggested layout starts from the beginning *(the left part of the display)* with the question and hypothesis, reserves the center for the equipment and results, and uses the right side for the conclusions. *(See FIGURE 3.13.)* If space allows, any of the equipment from the experiment can be displayed by placing it on the table in front of the display boards. The information taped to the boards can consist of drawings, photographs, charts, graphs, and so on. Photographs taken at various stages of the experiment add to the display, and sketches made along the way are also effective. It is not a good idea to display long written pages of information on the board. The display should have headings with large letters and short statements for the question, hypothesis, results, and conclusions. While all of the details of the project will generally not be included in the display, the sense of the experiment, what was done and what happened, should be clear.

Students often ask: How important is the look of the display?
The answer is simple: Quite important.

The display is part of the communication. It gives the viewers a feeling of how the experiment was done. Consequently, it is important for the student to:

- Be neat;
- Take time to make clear, simple, and neat drawings, graphs, and so on;
- Be orderly about the material;
- Avoid cluttering the display; and
- If possible, add little extra touches like lines of color, borders, and so on, to make the overall display look attractive.

None of the materials in the display needs to look professional. In fact, this type of a display is sometimes a drawback if the judges believe that there has been too much parental assistance. The more that is done by the student the better, but neatness is the key.

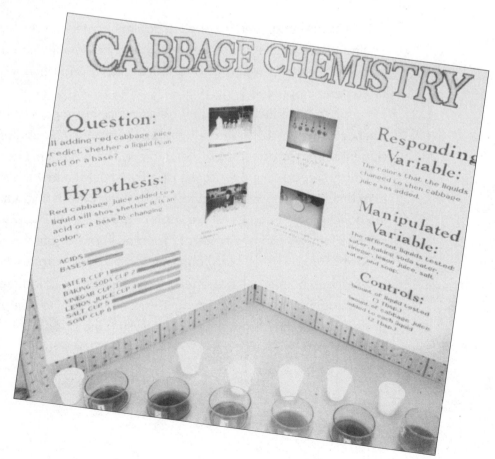

There are some people who feel that the display itself should not be very important when judging the project, that the work is more important than the display. In our fair, a display can receive a maximum of only 5 points out of 80. However, as a means of communication, a display can influence the judges' overall feelings for the experiment and the way in which it was done.

Students should be reminded of a couple of tips that have proved helpful:

- Check the spelling carefully. Misspelled words on the display give the impression that time and care were not taken to make sure that things were right, and errors reflects poorly on the experiment itself.
- Plan the display before putting it together, perhaps by making sketches showing the graphs, charts, titles and so on, arranged in different ways. The student can then choose the arrangement that tells the best story.

BRIEF WRITTEN PROJECT SUMMARY OR REPORT

Scientists and engineers most often communicate with each other in writing about the details of their work. This communication usually takes the form of a report or a technical paper published in journals or conference proceedings.

We have included an introduction to this important form of science communication through the brief written summary/report each student prepares about his or her project. The written project summary/report, like the project display, should follow the steps of the experiment starting with the question and hypothesis and ending with the conclusions. Because of the span of grade levels involved in the science fair, we use two types of reporting formats: one for the upper grades (7th and 8th—reports) and one for the lower grades (K–6th—summaries). Both forms are brief and concise. By making the report unintimidating, we find that students are more likely to complete their projects when they are not dreading writing the paper.

Project Summary Sheet for Grades K–6 Summary sheets may follow the outline below. The questions may be used as headings and then briefly answered to make up the summary sheet.

1. What question did I want to answer?
2. What materials did I use in the experiment?
3. What did I do to answer my question?
   a. What did I change?
      (What is the manipulated variable?)
   b. What changed as a result of what I did?
      (What was the responding variable?)
   c. What things did I keep the same?
      (What controls did I use?)
4. What is the answer to my question? (What are the results and conclusion?)
5. What books or other information did I use in the experiment?

A sample project summary sheet for a grade K–6 experiment is shown in *FIGURE 3.14.*

Project Report for Grades 7-8 A brief project report may be organized according to the following sections:

1. Title page *(name, grade, school, and project title)*
2. Purpose: the question to be answered and the expected results *(hypothesis)*
3. Materials and equipment used in the experiment, including instruments
4. Procedure followed in performing the experiment
5. Results obtained
6. Discussion of results *(how or why things happened the way they did)*
7. Conclusions *(the answer to the question)*
8. Bibliography of books, articles, and so on, used in the experiment

The "story" told essentially follows the scientific method of the experiment. It should be brief and clear and include photos, charts or drawings. These figures may be duplicates of ones used in the display; after all, they both tell the same story.

A sample report for grades 7–8 is given in *FIGURE 3.15* for the garden hose experiment. Though this experiment could easily be performed by students in lower grades as well, it was chosen for the subject of a grade 7–8 report for illustrative purposes.

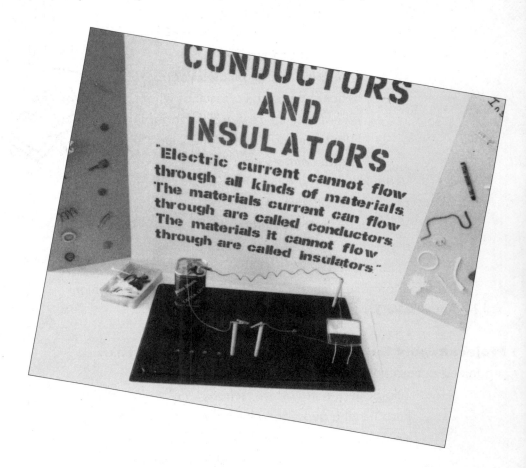

FIGURE 3.14   **SAMPLE PROJECT WRITE-UP: Grades K–6 Summary Sheet**

1. **What is the question I want to answer?**
    Which position of the weight makes the Geo-cruiser go farthest?

2. **What materials did I use in the experiment?**
    ▸ small weight   ▸ Captain Planet® Geo-cruiser   ▸ ramp
    ▸ tape measure   ▸ yardstick   ▸ tape

3. **What did I do to answer my question?**
    I did my experiment by placing my ramp in a particular spot. I then lined up my tape measure at the end of the front of the ramp about one foot away. I stretched out the tape measure, and I taped it to the floor. I placed the Geo-cruiser on the ramp with the two back wheels behind the very back edge of the ramp. I then picked up the rear of the Geo-cruiser a little and let it go down the ramp. I lined up my yardstick with the front of the Geo-cruiser, being careful to make sure it was straight, and I looked at the numbers on the tape measure. Then I recorded my results. I conducted the experiment 10 times with no weight, and then 10 times each with the weight in the front, middle, and back.

    a.   What thing did I change? Where I placed the weight: front, middle, or back

    b.   What changed as a result of what I did? The distance the Geo-cruiser traveled

    c.   What things did I keep the same? The ramp, the location of the ramp on the floor. I also did a test with no weight at all.

4. **What is the answer to my question?**
    The Geo-cruiser went the farthest with the weight in the middle. This was even better than with no weight at all. I think this is because putting the weight in the front or back puts more weight over the wheels and causes more friction between the wheels and the ramp. This slows the Geo-cruiser down and makes it stop sooner.

5. **What books or other information did I use in the experiment?**
    Gardner, Robert, *Ideas for Science Projects*. New York: Watts, 1989, pp. 72–74.
    Gardner, Robert, *Projects in Space Science*. New York: Messner, 1988, pp. 60, 62, 64, 65.
    Macmillan Encyclopedia of Science, Matter and Energy. New York: Macmillan, 1991, pp. 80-81.

    NOTE: Primary students do not always include graphs or charts as part of their project summary, but they are often included on the project display posters. The data and graphs for this experiment appear on pages in FIGURES 3.7–3.12.

FIGURE 3.15 **SAMPLE PROJECT WRITE - UP: Grades 7 - 8 Report**

1. **Title Page:** ————————————————————
   Name ————————————————————————
   Grade ————————————————————————
   School ———————————————————————

WATER FLOW IN GARDEN HOSES

2. **Purpose:** The purpose of this project was to answer the question, "How much is the amount of water that flows in a garden hose affected by the length of the hose?" It is expected that longer hoses will decrease the amount of flow, but by how much is to be determined.

3. **Materials:**
   - four 100-foot lengths and one 50-foot length of 1/2-inch diameter plastic garden hose
   - tall 5-gallon water container
   - watch with a second hand
   - basement sink

4. **Procedure:** I began by attaching a length of garden hose to the faucet on the basement sink with the water turned off. Then I opened the cold water valve all the way and let the water flow into the sink until it was cold and not changing temperature any longer. Then when the second hand was on 12, I placed the end of the hose into the empty container. After one minute when the second hand again passed the 12, I moved the hose from the container back into the sink. This procedure made sure that the water was flowing at full and steady speed for the whole minute; there were no differences among tests while the hose was filling with water.

   I measured the amount of water in the container by the water level and the 1/4-gallon marks on the side of the container. The container was 16 inches tall and 10 inches wide. Because of the tall shape of the container, there was a 3/4-inch space between 1/4-gallon marks, which made it easy to read the water level. I recorded these levels on my data sheet.

   I then emptied the container, changed the length of hose, and ran the next test in the same way. I was careful each time to lay the hoses around the basement floor in a circle with gentle bends. This procedure was a control to make sure that there were no kinks or sharp bends in some hoses which would reduce the amount of flow.

FIGURE 3.15   *continued*

The shortest hose length that I tested was 50 feet, and I increased the length by 50 feet up to 450 feet long. I also tested the flow for no hose at all. I repeated each test 3 or 4 times, and I used the average of the flow amounts as the best result for each length of hose.

5.   **Results and Discussion:** All of the measurements are listed in *Table 1*, and results are plotted in *FIGURE 1*. Each round symbol is the average of the amount of water measured for all of the tests with a given length of hose. The findings are similar to my hypothesis. The amount of water that flows decreases as the hose gets longer. In particular, I found that the flow decreases faster for shorter hoses than for longer hoses. The two lines drawn in *FIGURE 1* show the trends of the results. There is a change in the effect of hose length at about 150 feet. Adding hose to a short hose of less than150 feet decreases the flow of water noticeably. Each 50 feet of hose decreases the flow amount by about 3/4 gallon. For hoses longer than150 feet, each 50 feet of hose decreases the flow by only about 1/4 gallon. These fast and slow changes in flow are shown by the two lines in *FIGURE 1*.

TABLE 1	**DATA SHEET FROM EXPERIMENT**			
DATE	TIME	LENGTH OF HOSE (Feet)	AMOUNT OF WATER (Gallons)	COMMENTS
March 1	4:15 p.m.	0	4	Water was run 5 min. before test
March 1	4:30 p.m.	100	2 1/4	
		200	1 1/2	Water flowed through hose 2 min. at start
		300	1 1/4	
		400	1	
		0	4	
		0	4 1/4	
		0	4	
		0	4	
		100	2 1/4	
...	...	...	...	...
...	...	...	...	...
...	...	...	...	...
March 5	4:40 p.m.	400	1	Slight surge occurred during test

FIGURE 3.15   continued

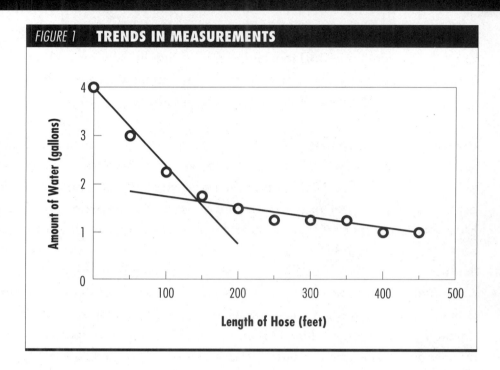

FIGURE 1   **TRENDS IN MEASUREMENTS**

6.   **Conclusions:**
   a.   As the hose gets longer the amount of water flow decreases, and the most change happens with shorter length hoses below 150 feet.
   b.   For the 1/2-inch diameter plastic hose used, 50 feet of hose added to a hose that was less than 150-foot long decreased the flow by 3/4 gallon in one minute. For hoses longer than 150 feet, adding 50 feet of hose decreased the flow by only 1/4 gallon in one minute.
   c.   The length of hose for watering a lawn is more important for small lawns than for large lawns. If less than 150 feet of hose is needed to reach all parts of a lawn, no extra hose should be used because it will decrease the amount of water that flows by a large amount. For large lawns that need hoses longer that 150 feet, the flow will be low, and extra hose will not lower it by much.

7.   **Bibliography:**
   Meyers, G. W., *Understanding Through Science*. New York: McGraw–Hill, 1990.

ORAL PRESENTATION

The display area will be quiet the morning of the science fair. When it is the student's turn to talk to the judges, he or she will be one of a few students in the area, so there will not be any distractions, and time can be taken for clear thinking. The student should prepare a short talk *(a few minutes is fine but not more than five minutes)* to explain the experiment to the judges. The talk, like the display and the report, should tell the story of the experiment and follow the steps of the scientific method. It is helpful to use the display in the talk. The whole story is on the boards. It can be used to remind the student of what was done.

The following steps are a good outline for a talk:

1. State the title of the project.
2. What question did you want to answer?
3. What did you expect to happen *(hypothesis)*? Mention books or articles read that influenced the hypothesis or other parts of the experiment here.
4. Describe the equipment, procedure, measurements, repetitions, variables *(manipulated and responding)*, and controls.
5. Describe and explain what happened; why or how *(results)*.
6. What is the answer to the question *(conclusion)*?

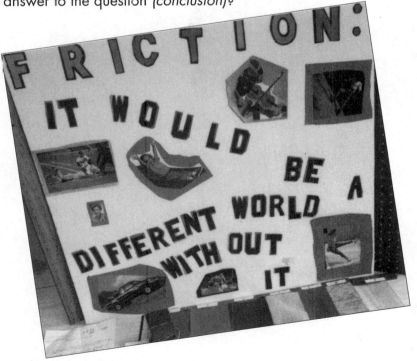

JUDGES' QUESTIONS

The judges will ask questions about the project. Typical questions may be about:

1. How or why the equipment was prepared as it was;
2. How carefully variables were controlled;
3. How accurately variables were measured;
4. How the experiment was run and records kept;
5. What would be expected to happen if something was changed; and
6. How much help the student had with the project *(What parts were done by the student?)*

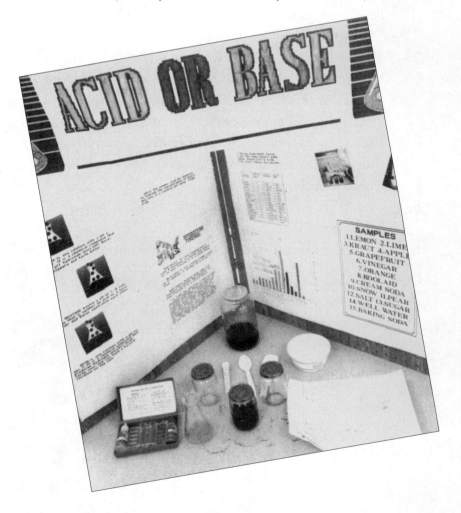

TIPS FOR THE PRESENTATION

- Thinking about the experiment and talking about it with others is good preparation for the student's talk to the judges. Students are encouraged to ask "what if" questions.
- It is fine for the student to let the judges know that he or she liked what was done, that something was learned, and/or that interest was developed in the topic.
- The student should try to relax, and speak to the judges like he or she might if seeing or meeting a teacher from school on a Saturday at a store.
- The student should think about a judge's question before answering it and be as clear as possible.
- If the full answer to a question is not known, the student should not guess but rather answer the part known.
- If asked to give an opinion, the student should base a guess on something related that happened in the experiment.
- Have fun!

4

JUDGING AND ASSIGNING AWARDS

The man who makes

the experiment

claims the honor and

the reward.

Horace

■ *All students who enter a project in the science fair win an award consisting of first, second, or third place. A first-place winner may also win a special "outstanding" award. In this way, all students are winners, and competition occurs only for the higher ranked awards. Endless hours have been spent on the issue of awards: Who are the higher award winners? What are the components of an outstanding project? How and why should various judging criteria be weighted? The purpose of this special attention to judging is to give all students an equal opportunity to achieve first-place awards by setting uniform judging criteria and*

by assigning importance to the relative scores rather than the exact scores assigned by each judge.

Students, parents, teachers, and community scientists put a lot of time and effort into the science fair experience. All projects deserve the fairest possible treatment in all matters and especially concerning judging and awards. By using the method of score analysis outlined in this chapter, the type of experience described below, so typical to science fairs, can be avoided.

A science fair steering committee at a junior high school was pleased with the large number of student participants. Appropriately, the committee had obtained the services of a sufficient number of qualified judges. Each judge was assigned eight (more or less) student science projects to evaluate. Groups of about twenty-four student projects were in competition for awards meaning that results from three judges were used together in determining project rank and assigning awards. Although all judges evaluated projects of comparable merit, the ranges of their assigned scores differed significantly. One judge gave scores as high as 99 percent while another judge assigned a highest score of 93 percent. The judges assumed that the scores would be normalized, since each had excellent projects to evaluate. This assumption was incorrect. The science fair committee simply took the raw scores from the three judges and ranked the student projects accordingly. As a consequence, only students lucky enough to have been judged by the highest scoring judge could possibly have received a first-place award that day. Considering the time and effort that both students and adults put into the science projects, they certainly deserve a better shake.

The computerized scoring method developed specifically for science fair use not only prevents this type of distasteful experience but also expedites the process of assigning awards. On the day of the fair, the time between project judging and the awards ceremony is rather short. In this time period,

approximately noon to 2:15 p.m., the important task of assigning student awards must be completed. The user-friendly computer program FAIR, included on the enclosed floppy disk*, allows this task to be accomplished expeditiously. The problem of the hard judge/easy judge is eliminated, and all students get the "fair shake" they deserve.

Each grade level forms a group in which awards of first, second, third place, and outstanding are awarded. The program treats each grade level separately. The averaged raw scores, as assigned by the judges, are typed into the computer. The scores from multiple judging teams at the grade level are normalized by the program, and the normalized scores for all students at that grade level are graphed on the computer screen. From this graph, the divisions among awards are established. Guidelines are displayed on the screen to aid in making these divisions. Typically, 15–20 percent of the students receive first-place awards; the same percentages apply to third-place awards, and 60–65 percent receive second-place awards. Outstanding award recipients are selected from among those students receiving first place awards for that grade level. The process is repeated for each grade level of the fair.

Individual judges typically evaluate a portion of the projects at a grade level, and there is usually not enough time on the day of the fair for judges to see the other projects at that grade level or any other projects in the fair. To rectify this situation, judges who are interested are invited to come to the fair location and preview all of the projects on the evening before the fair. The judges are offered the opportunity to leisurely review the projects and summaries/reports prior to the fair.

* If you bought this book without the disk, you can still purchase a disk separately from the store where you bought the book.

ASSIGNING PROJECTS TO JUDGING TEAMS

The week before the fair, the project reports and summaries are previewed by the Steering Committee. Based only on these reports/summaries, projects are roughly divided into three groups that appear to be above average, average, and below average. After project check-in the night before the fair, when all project entries are certain, these groups are used to assign projects to judging teams.

If there is more than one judging team at this grade level, the number of projects assigned to a single judging team should generally be between five and nine. The upper limit is set by time constraints on the day of the fair and the number of projects that a judging team can reasonably evaluate together. Higher numbers of projects, seven to nine per judging team, are normalized best by the computer program. You might assign as many as eleven projects to a single judging team at grade levels K–3, but at the upper grades, a maximum of seven to nine projects is better because the projects are more complex and judging takes longer. If there is only one judging team at any grade level, it is acceptable to assign fewer than five projects to the team.

The program FAIR will eliminate inequities of high and low scoring patterns among judging teams (tough judge/easy judge), but it cannot control the projects assigned to each team. The program assumes that each judging team has above average, average, and below average projects to evaluate. Selecting projects at random to assign to judging teams may achieve this distribution. However, since the number of projects per team is small, you can reduce the element of chance in achieving this distribution by grouping the projects. Using the reports and summaries for previewing and grouping projects, the task can be completed the week before the fair.

CRITERIA FOR PREVIEWING PROJECTS

The previewing process is a "rough" one since only one aspect of the project (the report/summary) is used. However, if the process is only 50 percent accurate, it serves its purpose.

> ▸ Projects that do not appear to meet the two criteria to be classified as an experiment *(see FIGURE 4.4)*—that is, they are missing a variable or a measurement—are placed into the group that is likely to be judged as demonstration projects.
>
> ▸ Projects that appear to be very complete in terms of all aspects of the scientific method (use of background information, use of controls, repetition of tests, and information determined from the results) or have a clear innovative component are placed into the group that is likely to be judged above average.

Two projects from the demonstration group are assigned to each judging team. Similarly, two projects from the above average group are assigned to each team. The program will perform properly if there is at least one below average and at least one above average project per judging team. Thus, if the judges' evaluations match the rough grouping half of the time, all will be well. If the grouping is less accurate than 50 percent, there is still randomness in the assignment of projects from the average group that can compensate for this situation. In eight years of science fair development, we have always used a previewing procedure, and the judges have always felt that the projects that they were assigned fell into all three categories of first, second, and third places. If, however, that should not happen, the program can still be used along with the judges' input to award only first and second places or only second and third places. This judging team would be treated separately from the others in the grade level. This special procedure is time consuming on the day of the fair when time is at a premium, and it is less desirable. Time is an important reason why we have chosen to preview and group projects before assigning them to judging teams. Also, when each judging team evaluates projects that receive first-, second-, and third-place awards, the program maximizes the fairness in assigning those awards.

It is important to note that the previewing process is not a judging process. It does not influence the judges' scoring and evaluating of projects. In fact, the judges need not know of the procedure used to assign projects to them. Previewing projects serves only to remove some randomness from the process of assigning projects to judges which helps in the fairness and timeliness of assigning awards.

JUDGING ON THE DAY OF THE FAIR

On the day of the science fair, judging activities start with the Judges' Workshop held first thing in the morning. Judging activities are complete after all awards are presented at the Awards Ceremony which is the last formal event of the day. All activities associated with judging on the day of the fair are listed in *FIGURE 4.1.*

FIGURE 4.1	JUDGING RELATED EVENTS: THE DAY OF THE FAIR
TIME	**EVENT**
8:30 a.m. – 8:50 a.m.	Judges' Workshop
8:50 a.m. – 9:15 a.m.	Judges read project reports.
9:15 a.m. –11:30 a.m.	Judges meet with students at preassigned times in exhibition areas to judge projects. Students make presentations and answer questions.
11:30 a.m. – 12:00 noon	Student judging complete. Judges have final conference with teammates and submit Science Fair Judging Sheets to Committee.
11:30 a.m. – 1:00 p.m.	Committee checks judges' addition on Judging Sheets, averages each team's scores, and posts average (raw) scores on Judging Tally Sheets.
11:30 a.m. – 1:45 p.m.	Raw scores are entered into computer by grade level. Awards are assigned and posted to Tally Sheets with normalized scores.
1:30 p.m. – 3:00 p.m.	Public viewing of projects
1:30 p.m. – 3:00 p.m.	Award ribbons placed on projects in exhibition areas
2:30 p.m. – 3:00 p.m.	Committee posts student awards from Tally Sheets to lists used in Awards Ceremony.
3:00 p.m. – 3:20 p.m.	Awards Ceremony

JUDGES' WORKSHOP

The Judges' Workshop must start promptly at 8:30 a.m. This event is the first of the day; if it is delayed, most things that follow will also be delayed. Since time is at a premium, adherence to schedule is important. Only 20 minutes are allotted for the entire Judges' Workshop, but it is an important starting activity. A sequence of events that has worked well for our Judges' Workshop follows.

1. Each judge has been sent a letter requesting his or her assistance at the science fair and specifying the date of the fair and the time commitment *(8:30 a.m.–noon)* *(FIGURE 4.2)*. They also are asked if they have a grade preference. Once judges agree to participate, they are sent a follow-up package of materials consisting of:

    ▸ A sample copy of the judging sheet *(FIGURE 4.4)*
    ▸ Judging Criteria *(FIGURE 4.5)*
    ▸ Judges' Instructions *(FIGURE 4.6)*
    ▸ The *Science Fair Handbook (APPENDIX A)*

Experience has shown that the judges can devise many reasonable interpretations of the judging criteria. In order to preserve uniformity, a brief elaboration on the intent of each criterion is included with the judges' package. *(See FIGURE 4.5.)*

2. All judges are asked to arrive by 8:30 a.m. Judges arriving early are encouraged to start reading the summaries/reports from the students they will be judging if they did not do so the evening before. Judges are introduced to their partners as they arrive.

3. The workshop begins promptly at 8:30 a.m. It provides the opportunity to "set the stage" for the day. A congenial, friendly atmosphere can be established by the presentation at this workshop. Remember that the concept of judging is a delicate matter in a science fair. The idea is to give students guidance in their pursuit of science, not criticism that will discourage them. The "tone" of the Judges' Workshop is important to establishing this atmosphere. Encourage the judges

to relax and enjoy themselves, and the students will, too.

Begin with welcoming comments made by a Committee member *(perhaps the Fair Coordinator)*. This should be followed by a concise presentation *(maximum length of 10 minutes)* in which the committee emphasizes items or procedures that are important to good and uniform judging. *(See FIGURE 4.3.)* Some of this information may be a repeat of written material included in the packages previously sent to the judges, but reinforcement of important items is appropriate. Judges also have an opportunity to ask questions and discuss matters of concern.

4. At 8:50 a.m., the judges either begin reading the written reports or reviewing other projects in the display area.

5. At 9:15 a.m., judges complete their reading of reports and go to the project display area to start the judging process.

All judging is done in teams of two: one teacher and one scientist. *(As discussed in CHAPTER 2, teacher judges are from outside the school district, and scientist judges may have science expertise in a variety of areas.)* Judges receive an individual Science Fair Judging Sheet for scoring each assigned project. These forms are filled out

individually by each judge of a team, but consultation between the team members is important. *(It is likely that the judges will not know each other and that most of them will be new to this community-based science fair approach, if not to science fair judging in general.)*

FIGURE 4.2   **LETTER TO PROSPECTIVE JUDGES**

February 5, 1999

Dear Prospective Judge:

We are writing to encourage you to join in our efforts to stimulate young minds in developing an interest in science. On Saturday, March 13, 1999, Valley Elementary School District and *(Insert name of parent support organization)* will be hosting its First Annual Science Fair, which involves the voluntary participation of students in grades K through 8. Thanks to the partnership of community volunteers and the school district, we hope to have successful fairs for years to come.

Because we need judges with technical *(or education)* backgrounds, we invite you to join us as one of our Science Fair judges. Judges work in teams of two composed of a technical judge and an educator; participation requires approximately 3-1/2 hours of your time on Saturday, March 13, from 8:30 a.m. to 12:00 noon. Judges can preview the projects and summary reports from 7:00 p.m. to 9:00 p.m. on Friday, March 12, and from 7:00 a.m. to 8:30 a.m, March 13. *(Attendance at previews is optional.)*

We are emphasizing the application of the scientific method in students' projects. Students are asked to do experiments, as opposed to demonstrations or collections. The overall intent of the fair is to nurture and develop inquiring minds through the application of science.

If you wish to join in this important endeavor, please call me or complete the information below and return it to me by February 15, 1999. Your assistance is appreciated.

Sincerely,

_____

☐ **I will serve as a judge on March 13, 1999.**   ☐ **I cannot serve as a judge.**

Name _____

Address _____

Phone _____

Best time to call _____

Grade level preference _____

FIGURE 4.3   **JUDGES' WORKSHOP PRESENTER INSTRUCTIONS**

1. **Review the Judging Sheet and highlight weighted scores.** Review the set-up of the Science Fair Judging Sheet, pointing out that judges should confer with each other but each is to fill out an individual sheet. Note how the weighting of some judging criteria is incorporated. It is very important to ask the judges to use the point spread on the Judging Sheets. There should be 30 points between an above-average project and a below-average project. In addition, remind the judges that the computer program that normalizes their scores uses a statistical algorithm that can be fooled. It is assumed that each judging team will have projects in all three categories: above average, average, and below average. If judges feel that the projects they have judged fall into less than these three categories, they should alert a Committee member, preferably the Fair Coordinator or the Computer Specialist. The judges should also write a note on their judging sheets indicating the special circumstances. It is important for the judges to "flag" this situation; otherwise the computer program will attempt to force their projects into the three categories. *(The Committee will have to deal with such an occurrence on a case-by-case basis. The projects for these judges should be entered into the computer program as if these judges were the only ones for that entire grade level. The program will generate a normalized graph from which one or two categories of awards can be assigned. The remainder of the grade level raw scores can be grouped together and entered into the program. Normalization among the remaining judging teams of that grade level will be performed in the usual way.)*

2. **Emphasize the need for fair-appropriate comments.** Emphasize the fact that the only written feedback that a student receives will be from the "Judges' Comments on Project" portion of the form that will be returned to the students. Remind the judges to be positive in their comments. They should be encouraging while addressing specific issues and avoiding generalities. Give them examples like: "The project could be improved by ensuring that the differences in growth measured were due only to the color of light applied and were not affected by the size of the seeds," not "The student did not properly use controls." Do not say, "The presentation was poor," or "The presentation was messy." Rather say, "The presentation should be neater, and all the results should be grouped together."

3. **Stress the importance of determining whether or not each project is truly an experiment.** Qualifications A and B at the top of the Science Fair Judging Sheet determine whether a project meets the minimum requirements to be classified as an experiment. If either item A or B is marked "no," criteria 2, 4, 6, and 8 will be given the minimum score of 1 by the Science Fair Committee even if

FIGURE 4.3   *continued*

the judge fails to do so as instructed on the sheet. Take care in applying these qualifications; a project that does not qualify as an experiment will likely receive no higher than a third-place award.

4.   **Review the roles of the judging team members.** Discuss the reasons for having both a scientist and a teacher on the team. Emphasize the need for teacher input on the grade level *(age appropriateness)* of each project.

5.   **Discuss the timetable.** Present the timetable for judging projects emphasizing the need to adhere to it because students will be admitted to the exhibition area on a preset time schedule. Project reports are read following the Judges' Workshop *(which must not run beyond its allotted time)* and before entering the project display area. Once in the project display area, judges will meet with students on a predetermined schedule as shown on the Judging Tally Sheets. Judges must be sure to allow a few minutes between students to confer with their judging partner.

   ‣ Judging begins at 9:15 a.m. and must be completed by noon.
   ‣ Allow 12 minutes per project for primary grades, and
   ‣ Allow 15 minutes per project for grades 4–8.

   Tell judges that students will be in the project display area only during the judging of their projects. This arrangement helps produce an atmosphere of minimal distraction and a quiet ambiance that is settling to the students. It conveys the important feeling that this is a time for careful thought. The atmosphere contributes much to pleasant student/judge interchanges on science.

6.   **Accuracy is essential.** The judges' exact scores are not important. However, as discussed previously, it is very important that: *(1)* each judging team has three categories of projects to evaluate: above average, average, and below average; and *(2)* the judges utilize the points available with a range of approximately 30 points between an above-average and a below-average project. *(As discussed previously, the assignment of projects to judging teams is prearranged by the Committee for the express purpose of ensuring that each team is assigned projects in all three categories.)* The computer program will normalize scores among judging teams at a grade level, thus eliminating the importance of the actual raw scores assigned by judges. Outstanding projects will be determined by point value alone.

JUDGING FORMS

The Science Fair Judging Sheet shown in *FIGURE 4.4* has been developed and refined over the course of many fairs, with input from a great many participants. Not only has the content received attention, but the layout of the form itself has also been scrutinized. Time on the morning of the fair is short, and it is important that judges easily recognize what they are asked to evaluate. The layout has been developed from experience in minimizing misinterpretations. *Note: In order to familiarize judges with the judging process, they receive copies of the Judging Sheet prior to the fair along with the explanation shown in FIGURE 4.5 in advance of the fair.*

MINIMUM REQUIREMENTS FOR CLASSIFICATION AS AN EXPERIMENT

In order to receive an award above third place, a project must be an experiment. Following the identification portion of the sheet, is the section entitled "Qualification As an Experiment." The minimum qualifications for categorization as an experiment are covered in question *A*: Were measurements made that allowed for comparisons?, and *B*, Was something changed or varied between measurements? If

a project does not meet *both* of these qualifications, the judge is instructed to enter the minimum grade of one *(1)* for four judging criteria *(numbers 2, 4, 6, and 8)*. This process will place the project in the third-place award category. If a judge answers "no" to either question A or B and does not enter the appropriate score of one, the Committee will change the judge's scores to ones *(1s)* on items 2, 4, 6, and 8 before awards are assigned. As discussed previously, this point is emphasized in the Judges' Workshop. The consequence of identifying a project as having either no measurement or no variable change is essentially to classify it as a demonstration.

A POORLY DONE PROJECT CAN STILL QUALIFY AS AN EXPERIMENT

The minimum qualifications for an experiment must be applied as they are listed on the Science Fair Judging Sheet in order to be uniform over all projects. Although satisfying these qualifications alone does not make a good experiment, it does distinguish an experiment from a demonstration. *(Turning a demonstration into an experiment usually involves adding a variable and a measurement as discussed in CHAPTER 3, Science Experiments.)* The following two projects created considerable discussion at one fair:

The student projects were titled, "Which Popcorn Pops the Best?" and "Which Paper Towel Is the Strongest?" Both appeared to be quite simple and were executed in rather haphazard fashions. Judges were initially too quick to label them as demonstrations. However, careful application of qualifications A and B from the judging sheet, pertaining to measurements and variables, revealed that indeed both were experiments; they just needed improvements. In the case of the popcorn, several brands were heated and the best was determined by the least number of unpopped kernels. With the paper towels, the brand that held the most weight was determined to be the strongest. Both projects included manipulated variables *(brands of popcorn or towel)* and measurements *(number of kernels or weight)*. Both were experiments, but both sorely needed controls to determine whether the tests were really conducted the same way with each brand to determine if the results were generally valid. Moisture content was very important in both cases, as was the age and size of the popcorn, and the method of holding the towels.

Another difficult item to consider is visual measurement. For example, students who observe mold growth by visual comparison may need to use careful controls. Visual measurements are not an acceptable alternative for more accurate types of measurements when available. This situation must be considered by the judges based on the age and ability level of the student as well as access to equipment.

FIGURE 4.4   **SCIENCE FAIR JUDGING SHEET**

Place sticker here with student name, grade, and project number.

*Judging team*_____

Qualification As an Experiment

A.   Were measurements made that allowed for comparisons?   _____ (yes or no)
B.   Was something changed or varied between measurements?   _____ (yes or no)

If either answer is no, enter the minimum score of 1 for criteria 2, 4, 6, and 8 below. Use the weighting   factors specified to arrive at the final scores for each of these criteria, e.g. the final score for criteria 2 would be 1 X 2 = 2.

Judging Criteria   Score (1–5)*

1.   Quality of written reports, grades 7–8,
      Quality of summary sheet, grades K–6   _____

2.   Student found an inventive way to answer the experiment question   _____ X 2 = _____
         Check items A & B above to see if a score of 1 is required for question 2.

3.   Student made good use of available background information   _____

4.   Student planned and executed experiment appropriately in obtaining results   _____ X 3 = _____
         Check items A & B above to see if a score of 1 is required for question 4.

5.   Student recorded data in appropriate ways   _____

6.   Student repeated observations and used controls   _____
         Check items A & B above to see if a score of 1 is required for question 6.

7.   Student adequately described observations and recognized important occurrences   _____

8.   Student drew reasonable conclusions from the results   _____ X 2 = _____
         Check items A & B above to see if a score of 1 is required for question 8.

9.   Quality of oral presentation & response to inquiries   _____

10.   Quality of exhibit   _____

11.   Project represents student's own work to the extent appropriate forthis age   _____

12.   Degree of topic creativity for this age   _____

Total of final scores (maximum = 80) _____

*1= Needs Improvement, **2**= Satisfactory, **3** = Good, **4** = Excellent, **5** = Outstanding
      Make comments to students below. Please be encouraging and personal.

- -

Judges' Comments on Project

The best things about your project are:

_____

_____

_____

*Place sticker here with
student name, grade, and project number.*

Your project could have been improved by:

_____

_____

_____

TWELVE JUDGING CRITERIA

The second evaluation area of the Science Fair Judging Sheet lists the twelve judging criteria used in evaluating projects. These criteria cover all evaluative aspects and ensure that each one will be judged with the same emphasis regardless of the judging team. Below is the rationale for each judging criterion, a summary of which is mailed to the judges *(see FIGURE 4.5)*.

CRITERION 1: QUALITY OF WRITTEN REPORTS FOR GRADES 7–8 AND QUALITY OF SUMMARY SHEET FOR GRADES K–6

A written statement by the student about the project is considered to be an important part of the learning experience. Preparing a summary of the project for others to read is an integral part of experimentation in science. The written material also helps students focus on the overall project in an orderly manner prior to discussion with the judges. At the upper grades, a report format is used which need not be lengthy but should include the following basic elements:

1. Purpose: question to be answered and expected results *(hypothesis)*
2. Materials and equipment used including instruments
3. Procedure
4. Results and discussion
5. Conclusions
6. Bibliography

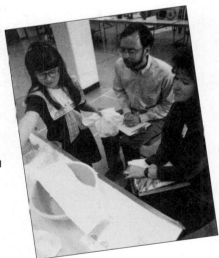

Typical upper-grade reports are three to four pages of written material, charts, and figures. At the lower grades, we have applied a simpler format which puts the whole experimental process in terms of a question asked, investigated, and answered. The content of the written material is much the same as at the upper grades, but the format is less formal and shorter *(typically about one page of writing accompanied by a chart or figure)*. Students provide a project summary that specifically answers these questions:

1. What is the question I want to answer? *(purpose)*
2. What materials did I use? *(materials)*

3. What did I do to answer my question? *(procedure)*
   a. What did I change?
   b. What changed as a result of what I did?
   c. What things did I keep the same?
4–5. What is the answer to my question? *(results and conclusions?)*
6. What books or other information did I use to help me? *(bibliography)*

CRITERION 2: STUDENT FOUND AN INVENTIVE WAY TO ANSWER THE EXPERIMENT QUESTION

Creativity in the project is covered in this judging criterion; creativity in the topic itself is covered in Criterion 12. *(In all, creativity in the project accounts for almost one-fifth of the total points available.)* Scientists and engineers are constantly in search of new methods, processes, and understanding. Creative approaches often lead to new and expanded information. Thus, creativity is given double weight in this criterion for a possible score of 2–10 points.

Since creativity is closely related to new innovations and knowledge in science, it is fitting that it receives a high point value. Typically, projects that receive outstanding awards at the fair have a unique and interesting topic or procedure. A routine project rarely receives an outstanding award no matter how well it is executed. *(The assignment of outstanding awards will be discussed in a subsequent section.)*

Criterion 2, as well as 4, 6, and 8, is affected by the answers to questions A and B. All four items deal with creativity, planning, execution, controls, results, and conclusions of an experiment. If the project is not classified as an experiment (either Question A or B receives a "no" answer), the judges are required to give the minimum score of one point to these four criteria. In that case, Criterion 2 would actually receive two points because it is multiplied by two. *(See FIGURE 4.4, Science Fair Judging Sheet.)* The weighting factors are always applied whether or not an item receives a score of one. The net result of a project receiving minimum scores for Criteria 2, 4, 6, and 8 is to almost assure the project will receive a third-place award.

CRITERION 3: STUDENT MADE GOOD USE OF AVAILABLE BACKGROUND INFORMATION

Work in science is usually a step-by-step building process. It is important to learn from previous work in the field. The purpose of this criterion is to judge whether the student made use of background material appropriate for the experiment and the grade level. The question "Does popcorn pop in oil?" does not require background information because the answer is common knowledge. However, to ask "How is popcorn popping affected by type of oil or temperature?" is a question that might lead to related background material not identical to the student's experiment. This information can be useful in guiding the experiment and anticipating results.

CRITERION 4: STUDENT PLANNED AND EXECUTED EXPERIMENT APPROPRIATELY IN OBTAINING RESULTS

This criterion is the heart of the experiment, covering the set-up and testing of the project. Careful work at this stage of the experiment leads to quality results. Due to the effort involved and its importance, the score for this item is multiplied by three on the Judging Sheet.

CRITERION 5: STUDENT RECORDED DATA IN APPROPRIATE WAYS

Students are judged on the appropriateness of the way in which they accumulated data. If the experiment warranted daily data recording, the judges should check to see that it was done. The experiment often dictates the best form of data recording, such as a table or chart. The accuracy of the data recorded is also a consideration. Recording the appropriate variables at important intervals contributes to quality results.

CRITERION 6: STUDENT REPEATED OBSERVATION AND USED CONTROLS

When attributing results to a particular variable, it is important to be as certain as possible that the variable used is the one responsible for the change. The student should be careful to control all but one variable, the one item being tested. Repeatability of results is another important condition showing that there is no unaccounted variable. The student should repeat tests or use a large enough sample size to be sure that results are accurate.

For example, growing a single plant which does not thrive in the presence of loud rock and roll music might lead to the general conclusion that rock music is detrimental to plant growth. It would be important to show that plants grow well with all other variables controlled *(water, light, soil, pot size, etc.)* and no rock music. In addition, many plants should be tested to show that the one plant did not die from some other cause. Other questions might arise. Was rock music the problem or, rather, just the volume at which it was played? Would classical music played loud enough cause the same result? Controls and repeatability of tests are essential in order for the conclusion to have any credibility. Thus, the topic of controls and repeatability is considered as a separate judging criterion. Since the question relates to the accuracy of an experiment, it receives the minimum score of one if an experiment was not performed *(if questions A and/or B are answered by a "no").*

CRITERION 7: STUDENT ADEQUATELY DESCRIBED OBSERVATIONS AND RECOGNIZED IMPORTANT OCCURRENCES

This criterion is related to the student's awareness of the developments in the experiment. If something interesting or unexpected happened, did the student observe it? The student is judged not only on the recognition of the major result of the experiment but also on the appropriateness of how the results were presented. Were charts, tables, and photographs used for the best presentation of results? It is important that the student recognize the important results and convey that information to others.

CRITERION 8: STUDENT DREW REASONABLE CONCLUSIONS FROM THE RESULTS

After the experiment is performed, the student should observe what can be generalized or concluded from the results. Drawing justifiable conclusions from results is an important part of any experiment. The conclusions should relate back to the purpose of the experiment *(the question asked)*. Conclusions represent the "bottom line"; consequently, this criterion is given double weight in the scoring.

CRITERION 9: QUALITY OF ORAL PRESENTATION AND RESPONSE TO INQUIRIES

Points are given for the quality of the student's oral presentation, including responses to judges' questions. Parental help is an important part of this science fair that extends down to kindergarten. Help may actually come from any family member, mentor, or teacher, but it is important that the student do as much as he or she is able. The student is expected to understand the experiment and be able to explain it and answer questions about it. The degree of understanding must be tempered by grade level. This criterion also includes knowledge of the exhibit in the presentation to the judges.

CRITERION 10: QUALITY OF EXHIBIT

Points are given for the display portion of the presentation. Neatness, clarity, and organization are key elements to consider. The grade level of the student should be the key factor in determining the appropriateness of parental help.

CRITERION 11: PROJECT REPRESENTS STUDENT'S OWN WORK TO THE EXTENT APPROPRIATE FOR HIS OR HER AGE

The appropriateness of parental work is a consideration in several of the judging criteria. Several of the judging criteria are phrased

"Student found . . .," "Student recorded . . .," etc. which is meant to emphasize the student's effort in the project rather than the parent's contribution. Criterion 11 provides points explicitly for the students who do their own work as appropriate for their age. A young child will certainly need more guidance and assistance than an older child. The parent should direct only as much as is needed and perform only those tasks clearly beyond the child's ability. For example, young students will often need help using tools or making measurements, but the adult helper should refrain from doing all the tasks. Lower-grade students will require someone to write the summary for them, but the student's ideas and words should be used to the extent possible while maintaining clarity. Upper-grade students are expected to write the report or summary themselves. They may seek assistance with typing. All students benefit from discussing the many aspects of their project with an adult. Topics include experiment idea, project set-up, results, conclusions, display, and oral presentation. Appropriate help that a student receives beyond discussions is a function of the age and maturation.

CRITERION 12: DEGREE OF TOPIC CREATIVITY FOR THIS AGE

Criterion 12 assigns points solely for creativity on choice of the project topic. This item is in contrast to Criterion 2, which addresses creativity in the procedure or methods of the experiment.

SCORING BY JUDGES

Scores for the Science Fair Judging Sheet are determined by the judges after evaluating the written report, the project display and discussions with the students. During the discussion time, the student should be asked to give a brief summary of the project using the display, if desired. Judges may ask questions on the understanding of the physical phenomena, development of the experiment and equipment, and "what if" questions based on results. It is important to everyone that the student know what has occurred, even if adult help was provided. Judges are encouraged to confer with each other after discussions with each student. Upon completion of discussions with all students, each judging team may wish to confer again and make some scoring adjustments to keep the relative scores appropriate. It is helpful to provide space, perhaps in the judges' room, or separate classroom, for such conferences. Finally, the judges are expected to enter the total score on the Science Fair Judging Sheet.

PROCESSING THE JUDGES' RAW SCORES

After a judging team has finished scoring, volunteers re-check the answers to Questions A and B on the top of the judging sheet and determine if the weighted questions were correctly scored. If a judge marks "no" to either question A or B, the volunteer is to change the scores for criteria 2, 4, 6, and 8 to one, even if the judges did not. They also check the addition of each score. These helpers average the scores of the two judges on each team and enter the results on the Judging Tally Sheet, *FIGURE 4.7. (Student labels will have been placed on the tally sheet according to grade level and judging time the previous night when all projects were checked in.)*

Judges' comments on the bottom of the Science Fair Judging Sheets are to be cut off and distributed to students with paper award ribbons and Participants' Booklets. Before this is done, the judges' comments will be checked for appropriateness of wording. Helpers may alter a judge's wording slightly without changing content in order to present criticism in a positive manner. The objective is to excite students about science and discovery. The comments should be viewed as recognition of strengths and identification of areas which, if improved, would have caused the project to achieve a higher score. In other words, judges are encouraged to tell the student in a positive way how his or her project could be improved. A comment like "the data recording was sloppy" should be rephrased to "more care should be taken with data recording."

When complete, the Judging Tally Sheets will have the average raw judging scores for each project at a given grade level. The tally sheet results are now ready to be entered into the computer program for normalization and determination of awards.

FIGURE 4.5   **JUDGING CRITERIA**

Individual Criteria on the Judging Sheet

1. Read the summaries/reports before viewing the projects and talking with the students. Do not judge an entire project based on your initial impression from the summary/report. Reserve judgment until you have visited with the students. In assigning points to a report, consider if the student has used a clear format, equivalent or identical to the recommended format. Is the student's summary of the exhibit clear and concise?

2. This criterion represents the creativity and inventiveness shown with regard to materials, schedules, measurement methods, and so on in performing and defining the experiment. This criterion *CARRIES DOUBLE WEIGHT*, consequently it is the *MAIN AREA FOR JUDGING CREATIVITY. (Creativity with regard to choice of topic is covered in criterion 12 which carries single weight.)*

3. Was available background information used in at least some aspect of the project? Sources could be books, articles, conversations, and so on. For example, in a plant experiment, was background information used to guide the planting, to review previously used controls, or to provide data for comparison?

4. This criterion represents the planning and execution *(the actual "doing")* of the experiment. It carries *TRIPLE WEIGHT.*

5. Did the student consider and record all of the appropriate variables? Was the interval between recordings acceptable? Was the accuracy of the measurements and recordings considered?

6. Were there replicate observations and reasonable controls? Controls are most often used to ensure that no more than one variable is changed at a time.

7. Did the student adequately describe the results using words, charts, graphs, and so on, and were the important features emphasized?

8. Did the student's conclusions follow logically from the objectives and experimental results *(even if there were scientific flaws)?* This criterion carries *DOUBLE WEIGHT.*

FIGURE 4.5   *continued*

9.   The best oral reports will adequately summarize the project and make good use of the exhibit. Consider the student's knowledge of the experiment and the exhibit as evidenced by the answers to your questions.

10.   The best exhibits will be self-explanatory. The exhibit should be neat, well organized, and attractive. *(Please review the instructions to students on this item.)* Consider the student's use of the exhibit during your visit.

11.   Did the student do most of the work? Where there was help from an adult, does the student understand what was done and why? *(Help with typing and complex aspects of construction is acceptable.)* *IF PARENTAL HELP IS CONSIDERED TO BE EXCESSIVE, IT SHOULD BE REFLECTED IN THE SCORES OF THE OTHER CATEGORIES THAT SPECIFICALLY STATE, "STUDENT MADE . . ., STUDENT REPEATED . . ." ETC.*

12.   Did the topic itself show thought and represent an interesting project? Take into consideration the grade level of the student.

FIGURE 4.6   **INSTRUCTIONS TO JUDGES**

1. Check that you have a *JUDGING FORM AND WRITTEN REPORT (for grades 7–8, or project summary for grades K–6)* for each project assigned to your team.

2. The five-point judging scale is: 1= needs improvement, 2= satisfactory, 3= good, 4= excellent and 5= outstanding. In order to better distinguish the qualities of the various projects, a spread of *25 TO 30 POINTS IS RECOMMENDED BETWEEN AN ABOVE-AVERAGE AND A BELOW-AVERAGE PROJECT.*

3. Each project will receive one of the following rankings: 1st, 2nd, or 3rd corresponding to above-average, average, and below-average work. It is assumed that you will have projects in all three categories. Because of the statistical nature of the computer scoring and the normalization of the scores that you assign, it is *VERY IMPORTANT THAT YOU NOTIFY US IF YOU FEEL THAT THE PROJECTS YOU JUDGE DO NOT INCLUDE ALL THREE CATEGORIES. (The actual values of the scores that you assign are not as important as the relative scores and the point spread among projects. The ranking is based on the total normalized scores of all projects in each grade level including results from other judging teams. Please use a 25–30 point spread to distinguish between above and below-average projects, and note that projects that you assign similar total scores will receive the same ranking.)*

4. Each judging criterion can receive a maximum score of 5 points. Extra points are assigned resulting in double weighting of criteria 2 & 8 and triple weighting for criterion 4.

5. Each team of two judges is composed of an elementary school educator and a scientist. Team members should consult with each other about the accuracy of the students' conclusions, the performance expected for the grade level, and so on. However, *EACH JUDGE SHOULD SCORE THE PROJECTS INDEPENDENTLY, NOT BY CONSENSUS.*

6. It has been our experience that time spent conversing with the students is very rewarding for everyone. We encourage you to ask questions of increasing difficulty, not only as part of the judging procedure, but also to establish a dialogue between students and interested adults. However, time is limited. Each team of two judges is scheduled to review 5–9 projects. Please *LIMIT THE TIME WITH EACH STUDENT TO 12 MINUTES (K–3)* and 15 minutes *(4–8)* so that students near the end of your schedule need not wait too long.

7. There are two questions to be answered by you near the top of the judging sheet. They relate to minimum conditions for each experiment. Please answer these questions after visiting with the student. *IF THE ANSWER TO EITHER QUESTION IS "NO," CRITERIA 2, 4, 6, AND 8 MUST EACH RECEIVE THE MINIMUM SCORE OF 1.*

8. Following the judging time with the students, you will have additional time to complete the *COMMENTS* sections at the bottom of the judging sheets. These sections will be returned to the students. It is the only feedback that they will receive (after the rankings are announced) regarding what areas to improve or what you may have liked about the project. Be brief, and list strong and weak areas. *PLEASE BE ENCOURAGING.*

9. The Science Fair is an exciting event. Enjoy your morning; the students will sense your feeling.

FIGURE 4.7 **JUDGING TALLY SHEET**

GRADE:_____   JUDGING TEAM #_____

JUDGES' NAMES:

. . . .

	STUDENT	TIME	RAW SCORE	NORMAL SCORE	AWARD 3,2,1–0*
1					
2					
3	Place label here with: student name, grade, and project number.				
4					
5					
6					
7					
8					
9					

*Outstanding

THE FAIR COMPUTER PROGRAM

NOTE: If your computer is a Macintosh, you can purchase the appropriate disk from the store where you bought this book. Documentation accompanies the disk.

This book is available with an IBM-compatible disk which contains the computer program FAIR. *(You can also purchase this disk separately.)* This program normalizes the scores of multiple judging teams in terms of both mean score and dispersion. The program will run on most computers that are compatible with a PC, XT, AT, or later model IBM microcomputer. It runs with most monochrome or color monitors. A math co-processor, hard disk drive, or printer are not required.

The program provides prompts for what to do each step of the way. To run the program, place the disk in the computer floppy disk drive. At the DOS prompt >, type the name of the floppy disk drive followed by a colon *(depending on which drive held the disk, you would type A: or B:)*. Then type the name of the file, FAIR, and press **Enter**. For example, if you are using floppy disk drive A, type:

> A:FAIR and press **Enter.**

Information Screens The initial screen that appears will ask you to identify your computer monitor as color or monochrome. Press **C** or **c** for color or press **M** or **m** for monochrome.

You will proceed immediately to the next screen, which provides general information concerning the functions performed by the program: normalizing scores, graphing scores, and providing guidelines for assigning project awards. At the bottom of the screen, you are given the option to proceed to the next information screen *(press 2)*, or to skip this screen and proceed directly to data entry *(press 1)*. The function screen explains that all raw scores for all judges at a grade level will be normalized to a range of 0 to 100 percent. The mean scores from each judging team will be equalized as will a measure of the dispersion of the scores. The input to the program *(raw scores)* is the average of the scores of the two judges for each student project. The output is a table of normalized scores and a graph of these scores. Awards are assigned based on this graph. This screen also offers options. You can view a final information screen by pressing **2**; press **1** to skip the screen and start entering data.

The final information screen explains the necessity for each judging team to have judged average, above-average, and below-average projects. Instructions are given if this situation does not exist. This screen also explains the use of the graph in assigning awards to student projects. You will be reminded that normalized project scores from all judging teams at one grade level are plotted in 2% bars, and three lines are also plotted on the graph. (See FIGURE 4.14). One line is plotted at the mean value of all the normalized scores for the grade level. Award division lines are plotted at the mean plus and minus one standard deviation. A reasonable distribution of awards is:

First Place: projects scoring above the line of the mean
                         plus one standard deviation
Second Place: projects between the lines of the mean plus
                         and minus one standard deviation
Third Place: projects scoring below the line of the mean
                         minus one standard deviation

Projects scoring within 2% of each other (adjacent bars on the graph) should generally receive the same award. If this occurs at the division line between first and second place, both projects should be awarded first place, even though one project is on or just below the first-place line. This practice will boost the number of first-place awards towards 20 percent, which is desirable. Similarly, adjacent scores at the second-/third-place division line should receive a second-place award. There are no adjacent bars in FIGURE 4.14 occurring at the division lines so that awards should be assigned according to these lines. When there is a large enough number of projects so that bars occur at nearly all levels, the division lines must be considered rigidly.

The subject of outstanding awards is discussed in a later section. However, one method of assigning these awards is to consider the first-place projects shown on the graph. A break between the highest scores and the others can be used as the criterion for separating outstanding projects from the remainder of the first- place projects.

When you are finished viewing the final information screen, press any key. You will move immediately to the data input screen.

Data Input Screens There are four or more input screens, depending on the number of judging teams at the grade level considered. The first data input screen prompts you to enter three parameters:

1. The program deals with one grade level at a time. First enter the grade level *(1, 2, etc., or K for kindergarten)*. Then press the **Enter** key as indicated on the screen.

2. A perfect raw score is 80 points according to the judging criteria and weighting discussed previously. If you modify the Science Fair Judging Sheet, you could have a different maximum score. When prompted by the program, enter the new maximum or press the **Enter** key to invoke the default value of 80.

3. You will be prompted to enter the number of judging teams for this grade level. Type the number, and press **Enter**, or press the **Enter** key to invoke the default of one judging team. This program was developed from science fair experiences where the number of judging teams were generally between one and five for each grade level. However, the program can accommodate up to 50 judging teams at a grade level. This large limit was incorporated to include a large number of projects that might be submitted, for example, from a large junior high school where all students participate in the science fair.

Entering Information Incorrectly If you enter information incorrectly, you may see an error message on the screen:

Redo from start

In this case, you need only retype the last entry that the computer did not accept. If for some reason you wish to stop the program before normal completion, pressing the **Control** and **c** keys together will stop the scoring program in many places.

Entering Raw Scores The next input screen calls for the entry of raw averaged scores. First you will be asked to type the number of projects for judging team number 1. *(The program allows the number of projects for a single judging team to be between two* *and nineteen.)* Judging teams are numbered to reflect grade level and team number. For example, three judging teams for second grade would be numbered 2A, 2B, and 2C.

The program will proceed to prompt you to enter the raw score average for each project evaluated by Judging Team 1, referring to Team A. *(Remember that these scores have already been averaged from the two scores assigned to each project by the two judges of a team.)* The raw score average will either be a whole number or will end in .5 as a result of the averaging process *(see FIGURE 4.8)*. The range of acceptable scores is displayed on the screen as a reminder. Typing a score larger than the maximum raw score entered on data entry screen 1 will cause the computer to invalidate the entry and wait for a re-entry.

You must press **Enter** after typing each score. If you catch a mistake before you press the **Enter** key, use the arrow keys to move the cursor, and change the score. You will have another chance to correct entries after all scores for Judging Team 1 are completed.

FIGURE 4.8	**FAIR RAW SCORE ENTRIES**
PROJECT #	TYPE RAW SCORE *(0–80)* AND PRESS ENTER
1	34
2	76.5
3	_Blinking, waiting for entry
4	

Changing Raw Entries Once you have entered all the raw scores for Judging Team 1, the program will re-display these scores and ask if you wish to make a change as shown in *FIGURE 4.9*. Press **Y** or **y** to correct an entry. Enter the number of the project, a comma, and the new score. *(For example; typing 4,50 changes the score to 50 for project number 4.)* Then press **Enter**. You will be prompted for another change. If you make an entry out of range of the raw scores, the computer will display:

** out of range **

The entry will be invalidated, and you will be asked if you wish to make another score change. When you are finished making changes, press **N** or **n**.

> *NOTE: Make sure that all entries are correct before pressing **N** or **n**. You will not be able to make any more changes to Judging Team 1 scores after this entry.*

FIGURE 4.9	**FAIR JUDGING TEAM 1 RAW SCORES**

Grade = 2
Judging Team = 1

PROJECT #	RAW SCORE *(0–80)*
1	34
2	76.5
3	78
4	40
5	55
6	61
7	64.5

Change any raw score?
Type Y or N and press enter.

Data Output Screens: The Table of Normalized Scores

After entering all of the raw scores for a given grade level, the program will display a table of normalized scores for all projects at this grade level as shown in *FIGURE 4.10*. The scores are listed by judging team in the order in which they were input. The list may take more than one screen.

Copy the scores from the first screen to the tally sheets for this grade level. You will be prompted to view successive screens. Continue copying normalized scores, in order, to the tally sheets until all scores have been copied. The next screen will be a graph of the scores. You will be able to view the table again later if you wish.

FIGURE 4.10	**FAIR NORMALIZED SCORES**

Copy scores to Grade 2 Tally Sheet before leaving this screen.

JUDGE #	PROJECT #	NORMALIZED SCORE (0–100%)
1	1	41.6
1	2	94.7
1	3	96.6
1	4	49.1
1	5	67.8
1	6	75.3
1	7	79.7
2	1	45.3
2	2	60.1
2	3	99.1
2	......	......

Press any key to continue.

Graph of Normalized Scores and Assignment of Awards

The bar graph that will appear on your screen will display all normalized scores for this grade level. The bars represent 2% score bands, and they are plotted against the number of projects receiving a score in that band. The graph is similar to *FIGURE 4.14*. For example, a bar above the score of 82 represents the number of students scoring between 80 and 82. The number of projects on the screen vertical axis ranges from 0 to 7+ *(7+ represents seven or more projects)*.

The vertical dotted lines shown on the graph represent the mean normalized score for the grade level and the mean score plus and minus one standard deviation. The values of these lines are also printed on the screen. Use these as guides for assigning awards—first, second, and third place, as shown in *FIGURE 4.14*. When you have determined the awards for the projects, write them on the Judging Tally Sheets.

Review Normalized Score Table and Graph, Process Another Grade Level or End the Code

From the graph, you can either return to the normalized score table or terminate this grade level by typing **N** or **n**. Finally, you will be asked if you wish to process another grade level or terminate the program. You can always restart the program from the DOS prompt as discussed previously. *However, once you leave the graph without recycling to the table of scores, that grade level is complete and you cannot return to view those scores again.*

AN EXAMPLE OF TWO JUDGING TEAMS

RAW SCORES

Let's see a sample set of scores in a case of two judging teams working at one grade level. Judging Team 1 evaluated eight projects; the raw score averages of their scores are shown in *FIGURE 4.11*. The scores were entered into the program under data entry. The bars shown in *FIGURE 4.11* are like the display you will see on your screen; they represent 2% score increments. The bar above the number 72 indicates that one project received a score greater than 70 and less than or equal to 72. From the raw score distribution shown here, it appears that the two projects scoring in the 72 and 76 bars would be awarded first place. One project with a score of 40 would receive third place. Second-place awards would go to the projects scoring 56 and 58. The two projects scoring at the 60 bar would also receive second-place awards. However, it is not clear whether the project scoring 50 should receive a second- or third-place award. Such situations of borderline scores are common at the science fair, and the normalization process performed by the computer program *FAIR* will provide guidance for determining the appropriate award for this borderline project.

Raw scores for Judging Team 2 are shown in *FIGURE 4.12*. Here the distribution indicates one first-, three second-, and two third-place awards. The project scoring 54 should receive either a first- or second-place award. Again, based on raw scores alone, it is difficult to assign an award to a project on the border between award categories.

RAW SCORE DISTRIBUTIONS FROM EACH JUDGING TEAM

There is a striking difference between the range of scores assigned by the two judging teams of this example. Judging Team 1 used the score range suggested and provided 36 points between above-average and below-average projects. Judging Team 2, however, provided a score range of only 22 points. In addition, the average score for Team 1 is 11 points higher than Team 2. These differences in mean and dispersion between the scores of the two judging teams is typical at a science fair. Such differences make it difficult to assign awards consistently for both teams without some statistical help as provided by the FAIR program.

RAW SCORES OF BOTH JUDGING TEAMS TOGETHER

If the raw scores from *FIGURES 4.11* and *4.12* were used directly for determining awards, a graph as shown in *FIGURE 4.13* would essentially be used. Assigning awards from this graph, one would likely identify two clear first-place awards and three clear third places. The break between second and third place is not clear. In this case, no students judged by Team 2 would receive a first-place award. This procedure does not work. It is a primary reason for the development of FAIR.

NORMALIZED SCORES OF BOTH JUDGING TEAMS TOGETHER—THE GRAPH IN FAIR

FAIR takes the scores from *FIGURES 4.11* and *4.12* and normalizes them relative to each other, considering both the mean values and the dispersions. The normalized results *(in the range 0–100)* for both judging teams of this example are shown in *FIGURE 4.14*. Three vertical lines are shown in the figure at the mean and the mean plus and minus one standard deviation. These lines are used as guides for determining awards as shown in the figure.

Note the adjacent scores of 60 and 62 near the mean in *FIGURE 4.14*. All five projects would receive second-place awards. Had these been adjacent scores of 74 and 76 at the division between first and second place, all projects would be given first-place awards. In fact, had the project that scored 76 in *FIGURE 4.14* actually scored 74, the two projects scoring 72 and 74 should be awarded first-place, even though 72 is below the division line. This grouping of adjacent projects at the division lines between awards is the fairest use of the program. Because of the normalization process, not only were all students from these two judging teams treated uniformly, but all students participating in the science fair received awards based on the same criteria producing a *fair* science fair indeed.

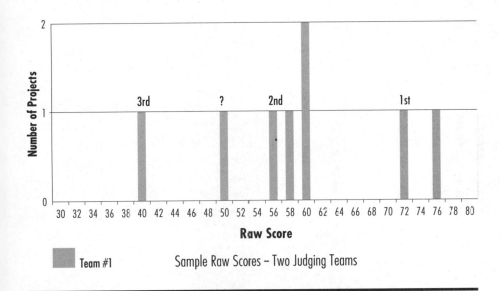

Figure 4.11 **FAIR EXAMPLE:**
Judging Team 1 Raw Scores

Sample Raw Scores – Two Judging Teams

Team #1

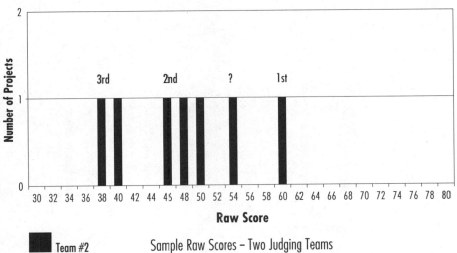

Figure 4.12 **FAIR EXAMPLE:**
Judging Team 2 Raw Scores

Sample Raw Scores – Two Judging Teams

Team #2

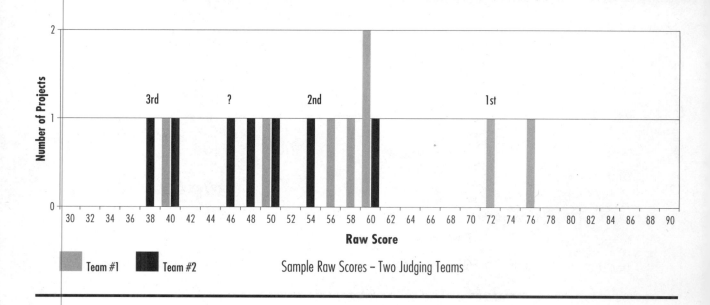

Figure 4.13   FAIR EXAMPLE:
Teams 1 and 2 Raw Scores Combined

Sample Raw Scores – Two Judging Teams

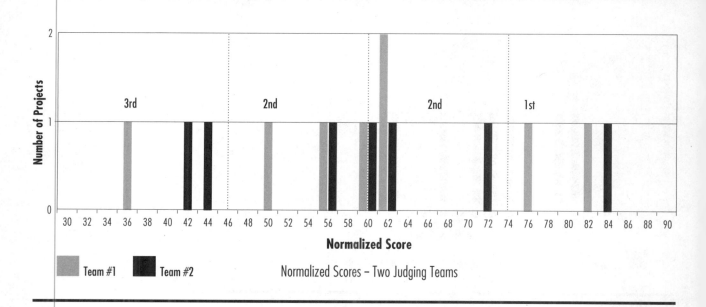

Figure 4.14   FAIR EXAMPLE:
Teams 1 and 2 Normalized Scores Combined

Normalized Scores – Two Judging Teams

DON'T FOOL THE PROGRAM

The program has been developed to be run without the need for information beyond what is given on the various screens. Some of the explanation provided in the preceding sections is repeated on the information screens of the program. At all steps of the program, the user is prompted for the appropriate entry or action. We have used FAIR *(or earlier versions of it)* successfully for many years. However, statistics can often be fooled, and you do not have to try very hard to do it.

1. Be sure that each judging team evaluates projects in all three categories, above average, average, and below average. Do this by having the Science Fair Steering Committee preview the Project Summaries/Reports the week before the fair. Based on a cursory preview, try to assign two above-average and two below-average projects and some average projects to each judging team. The program will perform fine if there is only one project in each of these categories, and trying to assign two per category compensates for the fact that the cursory previewing is not a very accurate process. This technique has worked well and has consistently produced the desired three category project distributions for each judging team. The project preview could be based on the displays the night before the fair, but it adds a lot of time to an already busy night, and it is not the recommended procedure.

2. Emphasize to the judges the need for a 30-point spread in scores between above average and below average projects. A somewhat larger spread is fine, but a much lower spread may fool the normalization procedure.

3. Keep the number of projects assigned to each judging team higher rather than lower whenever possible. A minimum of five projects should be assigned to a team when multiple teams are involved at a grade level. Seven to nine projects per team is preferable. A maximum of nine projects per team is a reasonable personal limit. Note that if there is only one judging

team at a grade level, any number of projects *(2–19)* is acceptable since the program serves only to graph the results for you. In this case, there is no relative normalization.

PROJECTS RECEIVING OUTSTANDING AWARDS

Outstanding achievement beyond the first-place awards can be recognized with outstanding awards. These awards carry the idea of "Best of the Fair." Not every grade level need have recipients.

Assigning outstanding awards is not an easy task. We have used several different methods and criteria for awarding them. One method was to emphasize the creative content of the projects and choose from among the first-place winners at each grade level. Two or three sets of experienced judges were used for this task. The judges re-reviewed the first-place project displays of entire grade levels and reviewed the comments of the original judges. This method used a uniform criterion for outstanding awards, but it did not consider the written and oral presentations. It was used for several years and has the advantage of finding truly outstanding projects from a creativity viewpoint.

At our fair, we have changed to a method preferred by a recent steering committee. The method relies completely on the computer code results. Using the graphs generated, projects whose scores are the highest in each grade level and stand out from the rest are assigned outstanding awards in addition to the first-place awards. This method bases the final determination of outstanding awards on the original judges' analysis of the projects, but it relies on the program to make small differentiation among projects. Using this method, the two highest scoring projects in *FIGURE 4.14* would receive outstanding awards.

Outstanding has been the most difficult award category to assign, and both methods discussed are workable. We find it valuable and continue to give about 10 percent of these awards each year. The students look forward to this part of the awards ceremony with serious anticipation and joyful delight when achieved.

5

Our ending is your

beginning.

L.V., D.M.F., K.M.P.

MAKING IT YOURS

EVERYONE WINS

■ *This book represents a labor of love, not only for the authors, but also for the scores of people who volunteered their time and talents over the past eight years. It is a tribute to their interest and dedication. The work of these individuals has brought us to the point where we are able to share the fruits of our combined efforts and the wisdom gained through our eight-year learning process. We hope this book helps you chart a course to a successful science fair—one that avoids some of the pitfalls that we faced in our initial efforts.*

We learned very early in the process that the power of partnership and the spirit of volunteerism increased the success of school science fairs exponentially. Our school district was able to hold a larger, multievent fair with the shared expertise of many school and community volunteers. Science instruction has benefited, and our children are much better off as a result. By using community resources to enhance the science fair process, the students are truly the winners. They observe their parents, teachers, school administrators, and community scientists working side-by-side to provide an opportunity for them, to explore their world through science. They see people other than teachers and parents interested in their work, discussing it with them, and applauding their effort. And they leave the fair with much more than a ribbon under their arms. They leave knowing their work is valuable. Their interest is piqued; they are encouraged, and they will return.

The importance of a steering committee cannot be emphasized enough. An undertaking of this magnitude requires that many individuals share the labor and responsibility. It also makes the effort of all involved much more reasonable, and the end result obtainable. The role descriptions and time lines found in CHAPTER 2, Keeping It All Together, give you a template to follow in organizing this facet of the science fair planning process.

We found that having a multievent fair was a must. Because of the size of the fair (seven schools in one school district), we discovered the need to "level the playing field" for all potential participants. Not all students would have a teacher with a strong background or interest in science. By holding Kickoff Assemblies in each school, providing a student/parent workshop and assuring the availability of liaison teachers in each school, we gave each student more equal access to the science fair experience. These events prior to the fair also enabled us to create greater and more sustained student interest in the fair.

Other science fairs allow younger students (especially kindergartners through third-graders) to enter demonstration exhibits. This is certainly a common enough practice. We would not discourage you from doing this in your fair at the expense of excluding younger students. We have found many benefits, though, from helping our younger participants learn and practice the scientific method. Give it a try in your fair. We doubt that you will be disappointed. Our experience with the requirement of experiments has solidified our personal opinion that it is the way to go for all science fair organizers. CHAPTER 3, Science Experiments, shared the basic steps with you on how to explain an experimental method in terms simple enough to lead the work of nearly any elementary-aged youngster. Don't pass up the opportunity to review APPENDIX C for titles of some unique experiments usable by grade school science fair participants.

You have read about our measures to make a fair fair. Refinements to the set of judging criteria have evolved with our experience with the fair. Having an educator teamed with a scientist has provided a real plus to the experience of our student participants. Providing a judges' workshop on the morning of the fair helps to further assure uniformity, but the greatest measure undertaken to assure this has been the development and use of the accompanying computer program to normalize student scores between judging teams. Holding a science fair competition for students brings with it the obligation to create an equitable contest for all students involved. While our primary goal was to provide a forum for more students to experience hands-on excitement with science, it was also important for us to recognize excellence in our participants' work.

We have found that occasionally a committee member or other volunteer with major responsibilities for the fair has felt burdened during the final stages of preparation of an event. Sometimes people have, at this point, questioned their willingness for future involvement. However, the day of the fair with all of the excitement about young students and science overshadows such thoughts. As with the students, the adults leave knowing their work is valuable.

You may use all of our procedures as we have presented them, or you may wish to make some changes to and adaptations of some of them to accommodate special conditions that you find different from ours. Four additional references that you may find useful are:

1.   Fredericks, A. D. and I. Asimov, The Complete Science Fair Handbook, *GoodYearBooks*, Glenview, Illinois, 1990.

2.   VanDeman, B. A. and E. McDonald, Nuts and Bolts, A Matter of Fact Guide to Science Fair Projects, *The Science Man Press, Harwood Heights, Illinois, 1983.*

3.   *You Be the Judge, Insights Visual Productions, Inc., Encinitas, California, 1988.*

4.   *DeBruin, J.,* Science Fairs with Style, *Good Apple, Carthage, Illinois, 1991.*

Also, make use of some of the many books written exclusively on science fair project ideas, equipment, and procedures. Good luck in producing your own fair, **not just another science fair!**

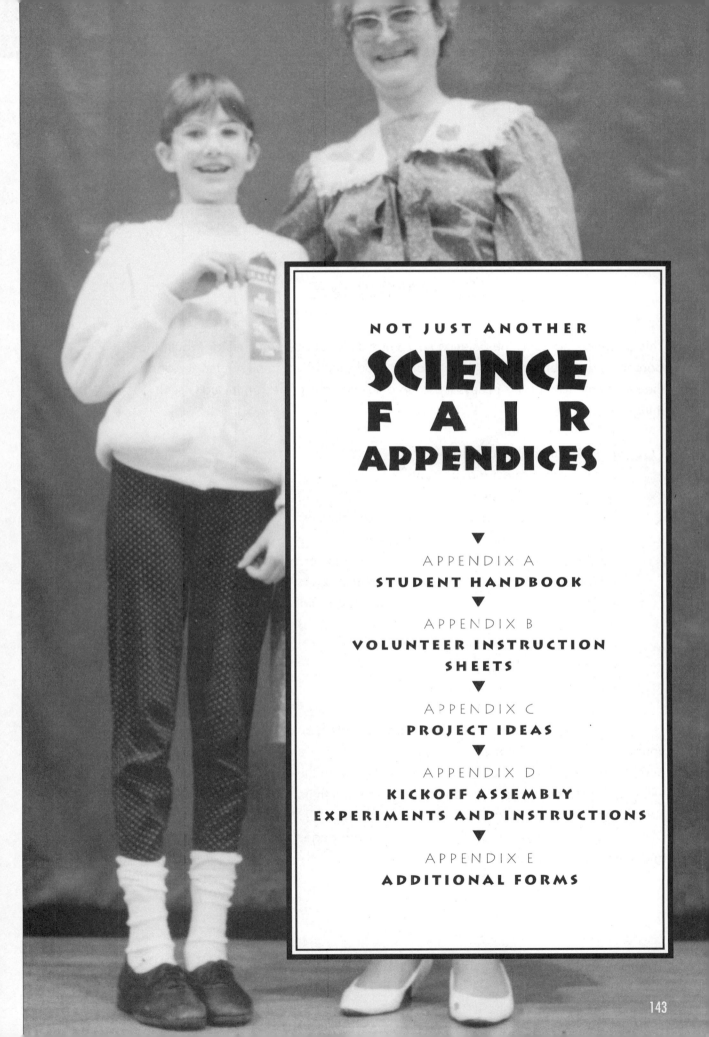

NOT JUST ANOTHER

SCIENCE F A I R APPENDICES

▼

APPENDIX A
STUDENT HANDBOOK
▼
APPENDIX B
VOLUNTEER INSTRUCTION SHEETS
▼
APPENDIX C
PROJECT IDEAS
▼
APPENDIX D
KICKOFF ASSEMBLY EXPERIMENTS AND INSTRUCTIONS
▼
APPENDIX E
ADDITIONAL FORMS

Appendix **A**

NOT JUST ANOTHER SCIENCE FAIR STUDENT HANDBOOK

This appendix contains the *Science Fair Student Handbook,* which is distributed to parents and students at the Student/Parent Workshop. It contains summaries of all the key elements that are necessary to do a science fair project. It includes such things as:

- Goals of the fair
- Important dates to remember
- Rules and project requirements
- Points on topic selection
- A scientific method for science fair experiments
- Sample topics for experiment projects
- Differences between demonstrations and experiments
- Project display guidelines and limitations
- Oral presentation to judges and sample questions judges might ask
- Guidelines for a written project summary
- Science Fair Judging Sheet
- Scientific equipment suppliers list

These pages are reproducible. Many include blank lines for you to fill in your own information before copying and distributing the *Handbook.* If you purchased the *Not Just Another Science Fair* Disk with this book or separately, you will find the *Handbook* in a file on the disk. You can then edit and style the Handbook as you would any text file in WordPerfect 5.1.

The Handbook can be duplicated on seven pages. Add a colorful cover and some clip art for eye appeal.

SCIENCE FAIR STUDENT HANDBOOK

Dear Parent:

The *Science Fair Student Handbook* contains information about rules, project guidelines, registration forms and other helpful items to assist in the science fair experience. A registration form is included with the *Handbook*. Additional forms and *Handbooks* are available from your school secretary.

Your cooperation in helping your child adhere to deadlines will help us do a better job of coordinating the fair. If you anticipate a problem with the dates and times specified in this *Handbook*, please contact us immediately.

Science Fair Liaison Personnel: Each elementary school has at least one liaison person who has volunteered to assist students in the planning and preparation of their projects if requested. These persons are:

_____—School 1
_____—School 2
_____—School 3
_____—School 4

For additional information, please contact_____.
(school district coordinator)

Sincerely,
Science Fair Steering Committee

See you at the fair!

SCIENCE FAIR GOALS

▸ To promote science education at all grades by hands-on exploration of scientific principles through the preparation and presentation of science projects.
▸ To promote understanding of, and creativity in, a scientific method of investigation.
▸ To promote the self-discipline necessary to accomplish the experiment, prepare a display, and write a summary within the given time frame.
▸ To give the students a sense of pride and accomplishment derived from participation in the science fair.
▸ To stimulate and nourish a fond interest in science.
▸ To promote educational links among parents, community, and school.
▸ To foster a lifelong appreciation of scientific processes in preparation for life in an increasingly technological society.

Science Fair Dates to Remember

_____, 19 ____ (six weeks before the fair):
Your project registration forms are due to the school secretary.

_____, 19 ____ (one week before the fair):
Your project summary/report is due. It must be turned in to the liaison teacher by ___ p.m.

_____, 19 ____ (night before fair):
Project check-in and set-up: _____ p.m. to _____ p.m._____ (location)

ABSOLUTELY NO CHECK-IN WILL BE ALLOWED AFTER 7:00 P.M. ON THE NIGHT BEFORE THE FAIR.

_____, 19 ____ (the day of the fair):
Science Fair Judging: _____ a.m. to _____ p.m._____ (location)

Public viewing and awards: _____ p.m. to _____ p.m.
Please try to stand next to your exhibit during public viewing so that you can answer questions.

_ALL RIBBONS WILL BE DISTRIBUTED AT THE AWARDS CEREMONY AT _____P.M. IN THE GYM._

RULES: ENTRY AND EXHIBITS

PROJECT REQUIREMENTS:
1. Students will not be given classroom time to work on their projects or write their reports. All project work must be done at home under parental supervision. Each school liaison teacher is available for assistance.
2. Students wishing to enter a project should fill out the enclosed registration form and return it to the school secretary by _____ , 19 ____.
3. Students must do their own projects. Each child will be judged on his or her knowledge of the subject.

   Parent Participation: Although one of the judging criteria is independent work, parents are encouraged to discuss the project with the student and provide assistance with research or preparation of the exhibit. Students should be encouraged to do as much as possible on their own. Students should do the manipulations and measurements in the experiments and should make their own drawings and charts. For younger students, dictation of the project summary is appropriate. Parents should advise their children about potential safety hazards.
4. Two students may work together as a team to complete a single project. However, if they are in different grades, they will be judged at the grade level of the older student. Each student in the team must fill out a registration form.

5. *Animal Experiments:* All science fair experiments involving animals must be in keeping with criteria established by the Animal Welfare Institute. If experiments are to be conducted on living subjects for science fair projects, then only lower orders of life may be used. Lower orders such as bacteria, fungi, protozoa, and insects can reveal much basic biological information.

   Vertebrate animals are not to be used in experiments for the science fair with the following exceptions:

   a.   Observations of normal living patterns of wild animals in the free living state or in zoological parks, gardens, or aquaria.

   b.   Observations of normal living patterns of pets, fish, and domestic animals.

         No living vertebrate animal shall be displayed in exhibits.

   Only observational type studies may be used in science fair projects involving chicken embryos. If normal egg embryos are to be hatched, satisfactory humane considerations must be made for disposal of chicks. If such arrangements cannot be made, then the chicken embryos must be destroyed on the nineteenth day of incubation. No eggs capable of hatching may be exhibited.

   Experiments involving humans or any other animals shall conform with these regulations. Normal physiological and behavioral studies may be carried out. Projects must be carefully selected so that neither physiological nor psychological harm can result from the study.

   Source: Animal Welfare Institute, P.O. Box 3650, Washington, DC 20007

6. Experiments with bodily fluids are prohibited.

7. All projects *(K–8)* must include:

   a.   Project display

   b.   Oral presentation

   c.   Project summary/report—Typed or neatly written.

   NOTE: There is a different Project Summary Form for grades 7–8.

8. The exhibit showing the results of the experiment may consist of the project itself, the equipment used, and/or pictures, drawings, charts, and diagrams. All exhibits must be durable and safe. Movable parts must be firmly attached. The actual display must be no larger than 30" deep *(front to back)* by 36" wide *(side to side)* and no higher than 5'.

9.   No flames or dangerous materials will be allowed at the fair.

10. Electricity will not be available at the fair.

11. All exhibits must be removed by _____ p.m. on the day of the fair. Exhibits not removed will be discarded. If you would like to display your project at your school, please check with your principal for details.

12. An identification number will be assigned to each project when it is checked in the night before the fair.

13. Absolutely *NO* parents *(even helpers)* will be allowed in the project display area after _____ a.m. the day of the fair.

14. Ribbons will be awarded at the Awards Ceremony held in the gym at _____ p.m. Photographs of Outstanding winners will be taken immediately following the Awards Ceremony.

15. The decision of the judges is final. The criteria given on the Science Fair Judging Sheet are used for all projects, and a computer program normalizes results before awards are assigned.

bE creativE There are many experiments familiar to adult scientists which are nevertheless new to children who are just beginning their work in science. These familiar experiments, when they are well done, make fine science fair projects. However, creativity is an important element of any science experiment. In a science fair, students earn points for using creativity in their choice of topic or in their approach to the topic. Students are encouraged to try a new way of testing something or to design a procedure in a better or unusual fashion. There are many new library books available on science projects, and often simple ideas can be tested in an unusual manner. Even if you are not sure a new method will work, the judges will appreciate your effort in thinking of something new and different. Such topics can make excellent science fair projects if they are done using a scientific method.

Selecting a Topic When selecting a topic you should consider several things:
1. You must be able to perform the experiment using a scientific method.
2. Demonstrations and models, while good learning tools, are *not* experiments. For example, a model showing how a human heart works is not appropriate.
3. Make sure the equipment you will need to do your experiment is readily available.
4. Consider the time needed to complete the experiment.

A SCIENTIFIC METHOD OF HOW TO DO A SCIENCE EXPERIMENT

A scientific method is simply an orderly method for investigating a problem or observing a process. A scientific method is an important part of the process of scientific investigation. While the results of an investigation are important, it is impossible to tell if the results are accurate without knowing how the investigation was done. Were the correct items tested? Were there controls? Was the experiment repeated with the same results? All of these questions need to be answered to establish the correctness of the measurements and the results.

All experiments must have two key parts:

Variables and Measurements There are three different types of variables.
1. *Manipulated Variable:* This is the one thing you will change in your experiment. For example, if you wanted to know how temperature affects the life of batteries, the temperature of the batteries being tested is the only variable that you would change.

2. *Responding Variable:* This is the thing that changes as a result of the changes in the manipulated variable. If you were testing the batteries in a flashlight, the responding variable would be the length of time the flashlight would work with batteries that had been kept at different temperatures.

3. *Controlled Variables:* Sometimes called controls, these are all the things that you will keep the same in your experiment. Controls in the battery example would be the brand and size of battery, the date on the package indicating shelf-life, the kind of flashlight used, the length of time each battery had been kept at each temperature, and anything else that might affect the results.

Measurements: By taking measurements of the responding variable, you know how much change has occurred. In conducting an experiment, it is better to measure changes that involve differences in time, distance, height, and so on—things you can measure in numbers. Sometimes, you may want to "measure" things by just looking at them and observing change. However, measurements in numbers are more satisfactory.

So, What Is a Scientific Method Anyway? Here are the steps:

1. SELECT A QUESTION you can answer by conducting an experiment. Use the library for ideas and information. You will find commonly done experiments, but you may also get some ideas about new topics and how to set-up your own experiment. Your question should be asked in such a way that it cannot be answered with a simple yes or no. For example, *"How* does salt affect the freezing point of water?" is a better question than *"Does* salt affect the freezing point of water?"

    Be Careful! Many library books suggest science fair questions that are really demonstrations. Make sure that you cannot answer the question with a simple yes or no. Also be sure that you will change something *(have a manipulated variable)* and measure something when answering the question. If you cannot figure out what you will be changing in doing the experiment, you probably have a demonstration question and not an experiment question.

2. FORM A HYPOTHESIS: This is a prediction about what will happen as a result of your experiment. Forming a hypothesis will help you design your procedure, and the experiment will prove or disprove your hypothesis. This step can be easier if you have visited the library and found other experiments that are similar to the one that you want to do.

3. PERFORM THE EXPERIMENT: Plan the details of your experiment. Select the manipulated and responding variables. Decide what things you must keep the same—these are your controls.
    a.   Determine what you will be measuring and what instrument you will use.
    b.   Select the materials to form the test equipment. Plan how the tests will be done:
            Which test will you do first?
            How many tests will you do?
            What will be recorded?
            How many times will each test be repeated?
    c.   Assemble the equipment to be used in the experiment.

    Prepare data sheets for recording measurements and for your comments. *(A logbook may also be used for comments.)* As you perform the tests, enter all measurements on your prepared data sheets. Take careful notice of what happens at all times and write down what you observe. It is important that you repeat each test several times. That way you can be sure of your results.

4. PREPARE THE RESULTS: Group and organize the measurements you have made. Make charts, graphs, and tables to show what happened. Wherever possible, use numbers to show your results. You may find that you will have to do more tests or perhaps make different measurements if you notice something happening that you cannot explain in one of your measurements. If one measurement is very different from all the others, check your comments in your logbook to be sure that nothing unusual happened to that test. For example, if you were testing the effect of temperature change on batteries and you dropped the flashlight, your results from that test might not be accurate. Try to understand the problem so that you can explain unusual results.

5. EXPLAIN THE RESULTS: It is a good idea to spend some time thinking about your results and talking to other people about them. Think about what the charts, tables, and your comments mean. Note patterns and amounts. Try to explain how or why the results came out as they did. What was the cause? Do the results agree with your hypothesis?

6. DRAW CONCLUSIONS: What can you say about your experiment in general? What can you count on happening again if someone else does a similar experiment? Again note patterns and amounts in your conclusions. If possible, try to describe how your results might apply to everyday experiences. For example, in the battery experiment, you might decide that it is better to store extra batteries in the refrigerator or freezer. Or think about what might have happened to the results if you had made a really big change in the manipulated variable.

Using all of these steps will make for an orderly experiment with reliable measurements and results. Follow this scientific method, and, like any good detective, you can trust your findings.

SAMPLE SCIENCE PROJECT IDEAS

Popular Topics

1. How does a certain type of fertilizer affect plant growth?
2. How does the amount of water affect plant growth?
3. How does the amount of water affect seed germination?
4. How does the amount of light affect plant growth?
5. How does the color of light affect plant growth?
6. Which paper towel is the strongest?
7. Which paper towel absorbs the most water?
8. Which popcorn pops the most kernels?
9. How is bread mold growth affected by light?
10. How is bread mold growth affected by temperature?
11. How is battery life affected by temperature?
12. How is magnet strength affected by temperature?

Topics That Are A Little Different Familiar experiments can be done with a new twist.

For example:

1. Rather than manipulating the variable of light by amount or color as in topics 4 and 5, manipulate its direction to answer: What effect does side lighting have on plant growth?

2. Instead of measuring the effects of temperature on a battery, measure the effect the rate of use has on total battery energy (if a battery will power a 2-watt bulb for 2 hours, will it power a 4-watt bulb for 1 hour?)

3. Experiments with flight are not often chosen. A parachute project that does not have an obvious answer is: What effect does the shape of the hole in a parachute have on its falling speed?

4. How does motion affect plant growth?

5. What is the effect of cigarette smoke on plants?

6. How is plant growth affect by watering slowly or all at once?

7. How much weight can be lifted by a string when the weight is lifted slowly? briskly? (Is a fish more likely to break your line when it is in the water or when it jumps?)

8. How is water flow affected by length of garden hose?

DEMONSTRATIONS

While demonstrations and models can help you learn many important concepts, this science fair requires students to do an experiment following a scientific method. Here are some examples of questions that do not require an experiment. They can be answered by reading a book or making a model.

1.   Can I grow bread mold?

This event can be shown by a simple demonstration.

2.   Do plants need light to grow?

This question can be answered by a simple "yes" or "no" and a demonstration.

3.   How does a battery work?

This question can be answered by a model or demonstration.

Do not pick these kinds of questions! Next we will turn these demonstrations into experiments. Remember, the judges will be asked to classify the projects as demonstrations or experiments.

EXPERIMENTS

The following examples are questions that can be answered by doing an experiment. These examples are popular topics of the type you may select:

1.   What is the effect of different temperatures on growing bread mold?

Manipulated Variable: Temperature

Controls: Light, moisture, kind of bread, location of sample

Measurement of Responding Variable: Amount of mold

2.   Under what kind of light do plants grow best *(grow lights, fluorescent light, sunlight)*?

Manipulated Variable: Kind of light

Controls: Kind of plant, location, moisture, kind of soil, size of pot

Measurement of Responding Variable: Height of plant

3.   How does temperature affect the life of a battery?

Manipulated Variable: Temperature

Controls: Kind and size of battery, type of flashlight, length of time battery will be kept at a certain temperature

Measurement of Responding Variable: Length of time the battery will operate the same flashlight bulb

NOTE: The judges will be asked to classify the projects as demonstrations or experiments. An experiment must have something that is changed *(manipulated variable)* and a measurement.

EXPERIMENTS THAT ARE A LITTLE DIFFERENT

Effect of light direction on plant growth

QUESTION: What effect does side lighting have on plant growth?

HYPOTHESIS: Plants may grow to different heights if light comes from the top, sides, or both. Top lighting should be better than lighting from the sides, but the effect of both remains to be measured.

VARIABLES:

MANIPULATED VARIABLES – Direction of light

RESPONDING VARIABLES – Height plant grows in a certain length of time

CONTROLS: Type of plant, length of time in light, amount of light, size of pot, type of soil, amount of water

Effect of use rate of battery life

QUESTION: What effect does the rate of use have on total battery energy?

HYPOTHESIS: Batteries tend to provide more energy when used slowly. The differences remain to be measured.

VARIABLES:

MANIPULATED VARIABLES – Size (watts) of flashlight bulb

RESPONDING VARIABLES – Time the battery powers a flashlight

CONTROLS: Kind of battery, kind of flashlight, age of batteries

Effect of the size of a parachute's hole on the time it falls

QUESTION: What effect does the shape of the hole in a parachute have on its falling speed?

HYPOTHESIS: Shapes that interfere with the passage of air should cause a slower fall if the chute remains stable. The differences remain to be measured.

VARIABLES:

MANIPULATED VARIABLES – Shape of the hole

RESPONDING VARIABLES – Time for parachute to fall

CONTROLS: Hole area, size of parachute, length of fall, shape of the parachute

VISUAL DISPLAY

Every student must have a visual display to accompany his or her project. Begin by making a small sketch of what you want your display to look like.

Things to remember about your display:
1. Your display board should be a self-supporting two- or three-sided display. *(See the RULES section for size.)* It may be constructed of posterboard, tagboard, corrugated cardboard, plywood, paneling, or pegboard, reinforced to stand securely on its own.
2. Lettering should be clear and legible. Stencils, precut letters, or large computer lettering are good choices.
3. The display should include the title of your project.
4. Graphs, charts, photos, and drawings add to the attractiveness of a display.
5. Use attractive attention-getting colors. Be neat and be orderly, following the steps of the scientific method in your display.
6. Do not clutter your display with unnecessary information. Tell a story. Start with the question, followed by the hypothesis, and equipment and procedure used, and end with results and conclusions.

ORAL PRESENTATION

Every student must give a short oral presentation to the judges. The talk should be a few minutes long *(five minutes maximum)*. When you give your presentation include the following information:
1. What is the title of your experiment?
2. What is the question you wanted to answer? *(Purpose)*
3. Before you did the experiment, what did you think would happen? *(Hypothesis)*
4. Mention any books or articles you may have read.
5. What materials and equipment did you use?
6. What did you do to answer your question? *(Procedure)*
   Be sure to tell the judges what thing you changed *(manipulated variable)*, and what thing changed as a result *(responding variable)*. Also mention those things you kept the same throughout the experiment *(controls)*.
7. What happened, and what is the answer to your question? *(Results and Conclusion)*
8. Be prepared to answer questions from the judges.

Here is a list of the type of questions the judges may ask you:
1. Please describe your project. *(Give your oral presentation.)*
2. Did you get the results you expected?
3. What caused the results that you found?
4. Would you expect me to get the same results if I built this experiment and performed it at my house?
5. Why did you build the equipment this way?
6. Did anything change besides the manipulated variable?
7. What might happen if you changed ...?
8. If you did this project over, what would you do differently?
9. Did you do the project yourself? If someone helped you, what did he or she do?
10. Could you do other things with this project next year?

PROJECT SUMMARY: Grades K-6

NOTE: *This summary must be turned in to your liaison teacher on Monday before the fair!*

As you develop your science fair project, think about the following questions. As you prepare your project for the science fair, write the answers to these questions so that others can know what you did.

At the top of the page place your name and leave a space for the number of your exhibit. Questions to answer:

1. What is the question I wanted to answer?
2. What materials did I use?
3. What did I do to answer my question?
   a. What did I change?
   b. What changed as a result of what I did?
   c. What things did I keep the same?
4. What is the answer to my question? *(Include any ideas that may have influenced the outcome.)*
5. What books or other information did I use to help me?

Your summary will be read by the judges. Please make it neat and readable. It can be as long or short as you like *(about one page is fine)*. You may use pictures, drawings, or graphs. These questions are another way of describing the scientific method for doing an experiment. They are meant to guide you so that your summary explains all of the parts of your experiment.

PROJECT REPORT: Grades 7-8

NOTE: This summary must be turned in to your liaison teacher on Monday before the fair!

An important part of doing any science project is documenting the information so that others may use it and learn from it. One way of making your findings available to others is through the writing of a project report.

This report is what the judges will read about your project. It is similar to your laboratory reports at school and can be as long or as short as you like *(three to four pages is fine)*. You may include pictures, drawings, and graphs if you wish.

Your report should have the following sections:

1. **Title Page:** The title of your project should appear in the center of the paper. Your name, school, and grade should be placed below the title.

2. **Purpose:** Describe why you decided to do this project and what question you were trying to answer. What did you think would happen *(hypothesis)*?

3. **Materials:** List the materials you used to do the project.

4. **Procedure:** Explain in a step-by-step way just what you did in your experiment. Remember, you want to describe what you did so that another person repeat it. You may include drawings if they will help you describe what you did.

5. **Results and Discussion:** Tell the reader what happened as the result of the procedure you used. You may use graphs, charts, tables, or a daily log to help the reader understand what you found out. This is where you discuss and interpret your results. Look over your results and write what you think the data show or seem to indicate. How did things change and what caused the results?

6. **Conclusions:** What is the answer to your question? Does it agree with your hypothesis? Can you conclude anything in general from your experiment? For example, if a battery temperature experiment produced the specific result that a D-size battery lasted one hour longer at a refrigerator temperature of 40°F, you might come to a general conclusion that common battery sizes AAA, AA, and C would also be expected to last longer at a colder temperature because they are all similar batteries *(how much longer would require testing of the smaller-sized batteries)*. Conclusions may include your opinions based on measurements.

7. **Bibliography:** List any books, articles, pamphlets, or other sources of information you used. Generally, follow this form: Author, Title. City where published: Publisher, Date. A book reference would look like this:

    Smith, John D., *A Study of Plant Life.* New York: Johnson Printing Co., 1989.

    A magazine article would look like this:

    Jones, Thomas A., "The Development of the Chick." *Animal Development Journal,* Vol. 16, June 1976, pp. 27–34.

8. **Acknowledgments:** Often scientists thank others who have helped them with their research project. This is the place to do so.

If you can compose your report on a computer or typewriter, please do; it will look neater. Ask someone else to read your paper before you submit it. Ask that person to look for ideas that may not be clear and suggest changes that will make your paper easier to read *(spelling, capital letters, and so on)*.

SCIENCE FAIR JUDGING SHEET

*Place sticker here with student name, grade,
and project number.*

Judging team_____

Qualification As an Experiment

A. Were measurements made that allowed for comparisons?   _____ (yes or no)
B. Was something changed or varied between measurements?   _____ (yes or no)
    If either answer is no, enter the minimum score of 1 for criteria 2, 4, 6, and 8 below. *Use the weighting factors specified to arrive at the final scores for each of these criteria, e.g. the final score for criteria 2 would be 1 X 2 = 2.*

Judging Criteria	Score (1–5)*

1. Quality of written reports, grades 7–8,
    Quality of summary sheet, grades K–6   _____

2. Student found an inventive way to answer the experiment question   _____ X 2 = _____
        Check items A & B above to see if a score of 1 is required for question 2.

3. Student made good use of available background information   _____

4. Student planned and executed experiment appropriately in obtaining results   _____ X 3 = _____
        Check items A & B above to see if a score of 1 is required for question 4.

5. Student recorded data in appropriate ways   _____

6. Student repeated observations and used controls   _____
        Check items A & B above to see if a score of 1 is required for question 6.

7. Student adequately described observations and recognized important occurrences   _____

8. Student drew reasonable conclusions from the results   _____ X 2 = _____
        Check items A & B above to see if a score of 1 is required for question 8.

9. Quality of oral presentation & response to inquiries   _____

10. Quality of exhibit   _____

11. Project represents student's own work to the extent appropriate for this age   _____

12. Degree of topic creativity for this age   _____

                                    Total of final scores (maximum = 80) _____

*1= Needs Improvement, **2**= Satisfactory, **3** = Good, **4** = Excellent, **5** = Outstanding
    Make comments to students below. Please be encouraging and personal.

- -

Judges' Comments on Project

The best things about your project are:

_____

_____

_____

*Place sticker here with
student name, grade, and project number.*

Your project could have been improved by:

_____

_____

_____

WHERE TO FIND SCIENTIFIC SUPPLIES

The following stores are good places to look for supplies.

NOTE TO COORDINATOR: Fill in this page with names, addresses, and phone numbers of appropriate stores in your area.

Appendix **B**

VOLUNTEER INSTRUCTION SHEETS

The instruction sheets included in this appendix are to be given to volunteer helpers by the appropriate science fair coordinators. They are intended to be a summary and a reminder to the helpers. It is expected that, in addition, the coordinators will spend some time with each volunteer discussing his or her part in the fair.

1. Committee Outline for Student/Parent Workshop *(see FIGURE 2.8 for a filled-in example)*
2. Project Review the Week Before the Fair
3. Set-up the Afternoon Preceding the Fair
4. Project Check-In the Evening Before the Fair
5. Final Set-up—the Evening Before the Fair
6. Telephone Answering the Morning of the Fair
7. Student Check-In the Morning of the Fair
8. Participants' Activities Room
9. Information Table
10. Escorting Students on the Day of the Fair
11. Distribution of Preliminary Awards
12. Final Clean-up

1. COMMITTEE OUTLINE FOR STUDENT/PARENT WORKSHOP

Science Fair Student/Parent Workshop

_____

_____, _____, 19_____, _____ p.m.

Theme: _____

Location: _____

Rooms: _____

Coordinator: _____

Arrival:

Lead-off Speaker:

Announcements:

Special Arrangements for Young Children:

Activities:

1. FIRST STOP:

2. SECOND STOP:

3. THIRD STOP:

4. FOURTH STOP:

5. FIFTH STOP:

6. SIXTH STOP:

Volunteers:

_____

_____

_____

2. PROJECT REVIEW THE WEEK BEFORE THE FAIR

The week before the fair:

1. Project summaries and reports are previewed by the Science Fair Steering Committee by grade level.

2. Committee members place 5 to 9 projects in groups for each judging team.

3. Projects are assigned to judging teams after a cursory Committee preview of the summaries/reports. An attempt is made to ensure that each judging team has at least two above-average and at least two below-average projects in the group. The computer program that normalizes scores among judging teams expects that there will be at least one first- and one third-place project per team. Thus, this project preview does not need to be very accurate *(nor can it be)*. This previewing process has worked well in assigning projects for each judging team that are above average, average, and below average. *This process takes some time, but it is very important to the whole judging, scoring, and awards process.*

4. After previewing and grouping projects for each judging team as described in item 3 above, place two labels on each of the two judging sheets. One label belongs in the upper left corner and one is for the comment section on each judging sheet. Paper clip the judging sheets together with the summary/report. Set them aside for assignment of judging times Friday evening.

3.   SET-UP THE AFTERNOON PRECEDING THE FAIR

Afternoon set-up, 3:00–5:00 p.m.
6 volunteers
Instructions:

1. Place colored tape on tables. Tables are color-coded by grade level. For example:

    K – Blue
    1st – White
    2nd – Red
    3rd – Green
    4th – Blue
    5th – White
    6th – Red
    7th – Green
    8th – Yellow

2. Use markers and tape measures to mark off every 36". You will also be given computer labels to place on the tape at each project location to indicate the project number and student name.

3. Make sure all directional signs are in place in display rooms and hallways.

4. Primary projects are located in _____.
    Intermediate and junior-high projects are in

    _____.

5. The table layout will be prepared in advance and given to custodians. Tables will be borrowed from all district schools, if necessary.

4. PROJECT CHECK-IN THE EVENING BEFORE THE FAIR

5:00–7:00 p.m.

> 6 volunteers: two at each check-in table, and two as escorts and project set-up helpers

At check-in tables:

1. Check each student's name off the list of participants.
2. Give the students a label to be placed in or near the upper-right corner of their display.
3. Please note any special requests for judging times. Every effort will be made to accommodate such requests.
4. Distribute sheet with the phone numbers to be called if parents wish to check judging times in the morning.
5. All science fair participants must exit the building by 7:00 p.m. There will be no check-in after this time.

Use of Student Identification Labels

LOCATION	PLACEMENT	TOTAL
2 per Judging Sheet	Upper-left corner & Comment Section	4
Display Table	On tape	1
Project Summary/Report	Upper-right corner	1
Project Display	Upper-right corner	1
Judging Tally Sheet	In order of judging time	1
Name Tag	On student	1
Awards List	Used in Awards Ceremony	1

5.   FINAL SET-UP—THE EVENING BEFORE THE FAIR

Friday night, 7:00–9:00 p.m.

All science fair participants must exit the building by 7:00 p.m. There will be no registration allowed after this time, with no exceptions.

1. Judges are invited to preview the projects at this time.
2. In the manner described, projects are assigned to judging teams the week before the fair. The order of judging is assigned at this time in order to accommodate parent requests to avoid time conflicts with other activities. The project labels are now placed on the tally sheets in the order that judging is to occur. The judging times are then written on the tally sheets. Judging starts at 9:15 a.m. with 12 minutes allotted for each K–3 project and 15 minutes for each 4–8 project.
3. The tally sheets with the project labels and judging times are photocopied and posted near the information table so that on the morning of the fair, parents may check their child's judging time.
4. A copy of the tally sheets with the judging times is posted outside the project display areas for grades K–3 and for grades 4–8.
5. Copies of all of these tally sheets are dropped off at the homes of the volunteers who will be receiving calls from parents regarding judging times. Five volunteers are needed to take calls the morning of the fair from 7:45–8:45 a.m.

6. TELEPHONE ANSWERING THE MORNING OF THE FAIR

Instructions for volunteers answering phone calls concerning judging times:

1. The sheets assigning judging times will be dropped off at your home after 9:00 p.m. on the night before the fair, March _____.

2. Students should arrive 15–20 minutes prior to judging so they will have time to check in.

3. *STUDENTS MUST BE PROMPT. JUDGES WILL NOT WAIT FOR A STUDENT WHO IS LATE UNLESS SPECIAL ARRANGEMENTS ARE MADE WITH THE FAIR COORDINATOR.*

4. Telephone calls should be made from 7:45–8:45 a.m. only.

5. If a reasonable request is made for a judging time change, please notify the Fair Committee, and provide a telephone number for the committee to arrange for the change.

6. For problems, concerns, and so on, parents can call this number after 7:45 a.m. the morning of the fair:

_____
(Phone Number)

7. STUDENT CHECK-IN THE MORNING OF THE FAIR

8:30–11:00 a.m.

2 volunteers

1. Check each student's name off the lists of participants *(on the copy of the Judging Tally Sheets)*. Lists are arranged by grade level and by judging time.

2. Do not rearrange judging times.

3. Use one computer label as a name tag for each student. Have the student place the name tag on his or her shirt and not on the outer coat.

4. Be sure students go immediately into the Participants' Activity Room and remain there until judging.

8. PARTICIPANTS' ACTIVITIES

The morning of the fair, 8:30–12:00 noon
1. Please check in with the Participants' Activities Coordinator upon arrival.
2. You will be assigned an activity to monitor.
3. Please keep children quiet while names are being called for judging.
4. If children ask to leave for a drink or to use the telephone or washroom, please remind them that they must return immediately. They are not to wander the hallways unattended.
5. All children should be finished with judging by noon.

9. INFORMATION TABLE

The day of the fair, 8:30 a.m.–2:30 p.m.

    3 volunteers, one at each time:

        8:30 to 10:30

        10:30 to12:30

        12:30 to 2:30

Post information that is pertinent to your fair. For example,

1. A timetable of events
2. Location of projects
3. Location of Judges' Room
4. Location of telephone
5. Location of bathrooms
6. Location and schedule of Participants' Activities Room. Include reminders that students will be supervised while waiting for judging and that all children must be picked up by noon.
7. Judging times are posted on doors. This schedule will be adhered to as much as possible.
8. Reminders that:
    a. No parents or students are allowed in the judging room until after 1:30 p.m.
    b. Parents cannot accompany their children during judging.
    c. Parents may wait in the Participants' Activities Room while their children talk with the judges.
    d. Public viewing is from 1:30–3:00 p.m.

9. A reminder: *STUDENTS ARE STRICTLY FORBIDDEN TO WANDER THE HALLWAYS. THEY WILL BE ESCORTED TO THEIR PROJECTS FOR JUDGING. THEY MAY LEAVE THE PARTICIPANTS' ACTIVITIES ROOM TO USE THE WASHROOM, PHONE, OR TO GET A DRINK OF WATER.*

10. ESCORTING STUDENTS ON THE DAY OF THE FAIR

The morning of the fair, 9:00–noon

    4 volunteers

1. All students are to wait in the Participants' Activities Room. They are to wear name tags with their name and project number. The first digit of the project number is the student's grade.

2. There will be a chalkboard and podium with a microphone in the room. Please announce the name of the student and then write it on the chalkboard.

3. If a child is not located, please go to the student check-in or information table to see if the student has arrived. If the student has not arrived, please have someone from the Science Fair Steering Committee try to call the student's home.

4. Please escort all students to and from the project display *(judging)* area. Students are not to wander the hallways unattended.

5. Sheets with assigned judging times are posted outside of each judging area and outside of the Participants' Activities Room. Please mark off the student's name from the appropriate lists as the student is taken in to be judged. This will provide a record of the judging.

11. DISTRIBUTION OF PRELIMINARY AWARDS

Award Distribution

Afternoon of the fair, 1:15–2:15 p.m.
1. Please check in at the judges' room upon arrival.
2. You will be placing construction paper ribbons, along with *Participants' Booklets,* evaluation forms, and judges' comments at the project displays during the community viewing time. The actual ribbons will be given to the students on stage during the Awards Ceremony.
3. The judges' decisions are final. Please do not attempt to defend the judges' position.

12. FINAL CLEAN-UP

Afternoon of the fair, 3:20–3:30 p.m.

1. Outstanding projects will be photographed prior to dismantling.
2. All signs are to be removed and returned to _____.
3. All projects are to be removed from the display area. Students are to check with their principal for display at their school.
4. The custodians will remove the tables, however, the tape should be removed and discarded.
5. Any projects left in the rooms after 3:30 p.m. will be discarded.

Appendix C

PROJECT IDEAS

This appendix provides a listing of science fair project ideas on a wide range of topics. In most cases, a project idea includes a suggestion for the responding variable as well as possible manipulated variables, any one of which could be used for a science fair experiment. The procedure, equipment, controls, and so on, are left to choice. Students can choose project ideas directly from this list and plan and execute an experiment, or use them as a starting point for others. Students should be encouraged to talk with their teachers, their parents, and members of the Science Fair Steering Committee to ensure that the projects they have chosen are appropriate for their age group, and can be done independently and safely.

The following five science fair projects all pertain to the corrosion of metal. The responding variable is given in the question; it is the growth or amount of corrosion. Suggested manipulated variables are wax, paint, varnish, silicone, or epoxy. Any one of these *(but only one)* can be used effectively in a science fair experiment. The details are not given, and that is up to you. For example, you might experiment with the type of paint, or the number of coats of paint. You can also substitute your own manipulated or responding variable for those listed. The method of testing is up to you, too.

How well is metal protected from corrosion by:
> wax?
> types of paint?
> varnish or shellac?
> silicone?
> epoxy?

Some of the project ideas that follow include a list of manipulated variables from which to choose, as in the example above. Others are single idea projects.

How is plant growth affected by type of water: tap, distilled, or lake water?

How is seed germination affected by:
- amount of water?
- salt content of water?
- temperature?
- acid rain?
- different fertilizers?
- different soils?
- vibration?
- rotation?
- electricity?
- amount of mulch?
- type of mulch?

How is the growth of plants affected by:
- humidity?
- type/amount/periods of light?
- type/amount/periods of water?
- turning?
- temperature?
- sound/music?
- type of soil?
- acidity of soil?
- soil mixtures?
- soil stratification?
- type of fertilizer?
- amount of fertilizer?
- very large amounts of fertilizer?
- electricity?
- cigarette smoke?
- salt content of water?
- vibration?
- rotation?
- orientation after germination?
- magnetic fields?
- different gases?
- caffeine?
- thickness of mulch?
- type of mulch *(plastic or organic)*?
- type of light *(sun or lamp)*?

color of light?

amount of light?

direction of light *(top, bottom, or side)*?

soap or detergent?

amount of various gases in the air?

How is seed germination affected by a pre-planting condition of:

freezing?

boiling?

microwave heating?

soaking in different liquids?

electric shock?

dental X-rays?

On which type of bread does mold grow more quickly?

How is the growth of mold affected by:

humidity?

light?

temperature?

How is metal corrosion affected by:

amount of table salt in water?

amount of other chemicals in water? *(such as Epsom salts or sugar)*

liquids?

temperature?

humidity in air?

acids like vinegar?

bases like baking soda?

type of metal?

surface condition?

How is electrical conductivity affected by:

type of material?

type of liquid?

chemicals in liquids?

temperature?

How is heat conducted through solid materials affected by:
> type of material?
> moving or still air at surface?
> moving or still liquid at surface?
> temperature of material?

How is heat absorbed from the sun or a sun lamp affected by:
> color of solid material?
> color of liquid?

*How does temperature affect the frequency that a
cricket chirps?*

How is composting efficiency affected by:
> amount of lime or other chemicals used?
> type of organic materials (food, leaves, and
> so on) used?
> amount of water?
> temperature?
> amount of air?
> light?

How is algae growth affected by:
> soaps?
> temperature?
> sunlight?
> amount of chlorine?

How is root growth affected by:
> soil type?
> vitamins?
> type of fertilizer?

How is fermentation affected by:
> amount of yeast?
> amount of sugar?
> temperature?
> light?

How is battery life affected by:
> temperature?
> slow or fast use?

How much is friction changed by:
> lubricants?
> temperature?
> surface roughness?
> bearing type?

How is the holding strength of glues, adhesives, or fasteners such as nails, screws, or rivets affected by:
> type of glue?
> type or size of nail or screw?
> material of rivet?
> type of materials being bonded?

How is the strength of fasteners affected by the way force is applied: pulling, pushing, twisting, sliding, or bending?

How is bending a nail until it breaks (fatigue) affected by:
> speed of bending?
> diameter of nail?
> material of nail?
> movement of each bend?
> temperature?

How long does food last when stored in different containers or encased by different food wrappings?

Which brand of popcorn pops the most kernels?

Which brand of paper towel or diaper:
> is the strongest?
> absorbs the most liquid?

Which brand of soap or detergent cleans best?

Which brand of stain remover works best?

Which type of packing material is best for protection against shock or breakage?

How long do various amounts of aspirin extend the life of cut flowers?

How is the speed of a model car or boat affected by:
   shape?
   weight?
   area?
   model car wheel bearings?
   water temperature for boats?

How is the dissolving speed of powders (like salt) or solids (like candy) affected by:
   stirring?
   heating?
   type of liquid?
   amount of liquid?

How is magnetic recording tape affected by temperature?

How is magnetic erasure of recording tape affected by:
   strength of magnet?
   distance from magnet to tape?
   temperature?

How is the height of a bouncing ball affected by:
   size of ball?
   height from which ball is dropped?
   temperature of ball?
   temperature of surface?
   material of ball or surface?

How is shoe traction affected by:
   pattern in the sole?
   sole material?
   weight of the wearer?

How is traction of a bicycle tire affected by:
>   pattern in the tire?
>   weight of rider?

How does baseball bat material (wood or aluminum) affect hitting distance?

How is parachute falling speed affected by:
>   shape of chute?
>   shape of hole(s)?
>   size of chute?
>   size of hole?
>   number of holes?
>   placement of holes?
>   material?
>   weight?

How is the stretch length of rubber bands affected by:
>   weight attached?
>   width?
>   length?

How is paper/model airplane distance affected by:
>   design of plane?
>   design of body?
>   design of wings?
>   type of paper?
>   distribution of weight?
>   amount of weight?
>   angle of launch?

How does terracing affect soil erosion?

How does temperature affect people's ability to taste differences in:
>   meats?
>   soft drinks?
>   sweets?

How is sail performance affected by:
> *shape?*
> *weight?*
> *material?*
> *size?*
> *angle to wind?*

How does the performance of a plastic or metal sail compare to a fabric sail?

How is lift of a model airplane affected by the design of the wing?

What are the differences in flight among model airplanes with flat and curved wings?

How effective are different sunglasses materials in blocking light?

How does cooking method affect the amount of Vitamin C remaining in food?

How does temperature affect the electricity generated by a solar cell?

How is the rolling speed of a ball affected by:
> *material?*
> *size?*
> *weight?*
> *angle of ramp?*

How good are air spaces of different thicknesses as heat insulators?

How much are fabrics damaged by:
> *pollutants in water or air (such as tobacco smoke)?*
> *sunlight?*
> *number of washings?*
> *type of detergent?*

How is the hardness of different types of wood affected by:
> moisture?
> temperature?

How is melting snow in sunlight affected by color?

How does food coloring in ice cubes affect melting in sunlight?

How is dough/cake rising affected by:
> yeast?
> temperature?
> sound?
> vibration?
> sugar content?
> salt content?

How is stained or painted wood affected by:
> sunlight?
> temperature?
> type of wood?
> type of stain or paint?
> humidity/moisture?

How is soil erosion affected by:
> rate of watering?
> slope of land?
> type of soil?

How effective are different types of automobile windshield sunscreens?

How is blood pressure affected by:
> caffeine?
> exercising?
> bathing?

Appendix D

KICKOFF ASSEMBLY EXPERIMENTS AND INSTRUCTIONS

Following are six experiments presented successfully in Kickoff Assemblies at each of the three grade levels. They work well because changes in the responding variables are easily seen by a group. The experiments are presented in student report format following the steps in CHAPTER 3. A list of instructions to the person or people presenting the Kickoff Assemblies is also included.

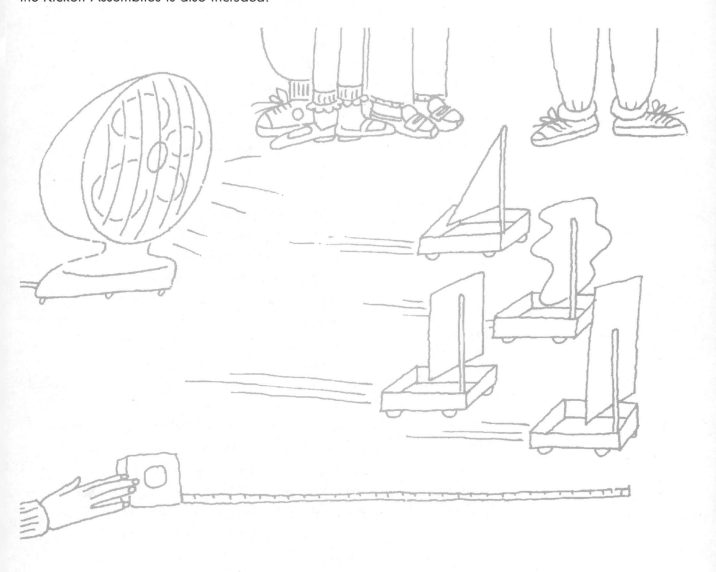

GRADES K–3

How Far Does a Rubber Band Travel?

1. *What is the question I want to answer?* How far does a rubber band travel when it is stretched different amounts?

2. *What materials did I use?* A board marked in one foot spaces, a large rubber band, a table, a tape measure

3. *What did I do?* I marked a board in one foot spaces so it looked like a big ruler. I rested the board against the edge of a table so it was always in the same position. I put the rubber band across the end of the board being careful that no one was standing in front of the board. I pulled the rubber band back 1 foot at a time and shot it. I used a tape measure to measure the distance the rubber band traveled. I repeated each test three times.

   Variables:

   a. What thing did I change? *(Manipulated Variable)* I changed how far back I pulled the rubber band.

   b. What changed as a result of what I did? *(Responding Variable)* The rubber band traveled different distances.

   c. What things did I keep the same? *(Controls)* I always used the same board and rubber band. I kept the board in the same position. I always measured from the same place to where the rubber band landed.

4. *What is the answer to my question?* The farther I pulled the rubber band back, the farther it traveled when I released it. The distance traveled changed the same way as the amount of the rubber band stretch. For example, stretching the rubber band twice as much made the rubber band travel twice as far.

5. *What books did I use?* Mandell, Muriel, *Complete Science Course for Young Experimenters.* New York: Sterling, 1979.

GRADES K–3

How Important Is the Shape of a Sail?

1. *What is the question I want to answer?* If I change a sail's shape, will it change how far a cart goes?

2. *What materials did I use?* I used a cart, tagboard, masking tape, and a fan.

3. *What did I do?*

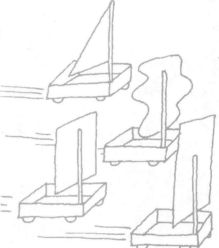

   a. I made 3 different sails out of tagboard. All 3 sails had the same area, but each had a different shape: square, triangle with equal length sides, and a long thin rectangle.

   b. I attached each sail to the cart with masking tape.

   c. I placed the cart, with a sail attached, at the starting line in front of the fan.

   d. I turned the fan on "high" and waited for the cart to stop moving.

   e. I tried each sail 3 times.

   f. I measured how far the cart went each time and recorded it.

   Variables:

   a. What thing did I change? *(Manipulated Variable)* The shape of the sail was changed.

   b. What changed as a result of what I did? *(Responding Variable)* The distance the cart traveled changed.

   c. What things did I keep the same? *(Controls)* I kept the fan, the cart, and the starting line the same. I also kept the size of each kind of sail the same. *(All three sails had the same area.)*

4. *What is the answer to my question?* It does not matter what shape is used for a tagboard sail unless it is very unusual. The square sail and triangle sail made the cart go about the same distance, but the long, thin rectangle sail made the cart go about half as far.

5. *What books did I use?* Mandell, Muriel, *Complete Science Course for Young Experimenters*. New York: Sterling, 1979.

GRADES 4-6

Launching an Object

1. *What is the question I want to answer?* How does the angle of launch affect the distance a dart travels?

2. *What materials did I use?* Large board, yardstick, masking tape, marker, dart gun, suction cup darts, tape measure, and paint were used.

3. *What did I do?* I marked a place on the floor for my launch site. I attached the gun to the yardstick and put a bolt through the hole in the end of the yardstick. I used a large board as a protractor and drew lines at 0, 15, 30, 45, 60, 75, and 90 degrees. I drilled a hole through the yardstick and the board at the zero point and attached the yardstick with the bolt through it. I held the board at the launch line and loaded the gun. I dipped the end of the darts in a little paint and shot the darts 3 times at each angle. I measured the distance each dart traveled and averaged my results.

    Variables:

    a. What thing did I change? *(Manipulated Variable)* I changed the angle of the gun.

    b. What changed as a result of what I did? *(Responding Variable)* The distance the darts traveled changed.

    c. What things did I keep the same? *(Controls)* The gun, the darts, and the launch line were kept the same. I also made sure there were no windows or doors open so that there was no wind to affect my results.

4. *What is the answer to my question?* The dart traveled the farthest when it was shot from a 45-degree angle.

5. *What books did I use?* Mandell, Muriel, *Complete Science Course for Young Experimenters.* New York: Sterling, 1979.

GRADES 4–6

How Important Is the Shape of a Sail?

1. *What is the question I want to answer?* How will changing the shape of a tagboard sail attached to a cart affect the distance the cart will travel?

2. *What materials did I use?* I used a cart, tagboard, masking tape, tape measure, and a fan.

3. *What did I do?*

    a. I made three different sails out of tagboard. All the sails had the same area, but each had a different shape. I used an equilateral triangle, a square, and a long, thin rectangle.

    b. I attached the sail to the cart firmly with masking tape.

    c. I placed the cart at the starting line in front of the fan.

    d. I turned the fan on high and waited for the cart to stop moving.

    e. I tried each sail 3 times.

    f. I measured the distance the cart traveled each time and recorded it. I averaged the distance the cart traveled with each sail.

    Variables:

    a. What did I change? *(Manipulated variable)* The shape of the sail was changed.

    b. What changed as a result of what I did? *(Responding variable)* The distance the cart traveled changed.

    c. What things did I keep the same? *(Controls)* I kept the same area of the sail, the same fan, cart, and starting line.

4. *What is the answer to my question?* The cart nearly went the same distance each time with the square and triangular sails, but the unusual shape of the long, thin rectangle only moved the cart about half as far. It does not matter what shape the sail is as long as each sail is the same size and roughly the same shape *(like the equal-sided triangle and square.)* I read about

sailboats, and I think that if more shapes were tested, more differences would occur. The experiment would be better because there would be many more measurements and shapes involved. This idea would make a good experiment for another time.

How could I change this experiment or improve it? I think that sometimes the distance the cart traveled was different because I did not line up the cart straight in front of the fan. Also, I think it would be a good idea to clean the floor and the wheels between each trial to make sure that no dirt is interfering with the cart. It is important to use a level floor during this experiment.

It would be interesting to make the sails out of cloth. Also, as I said before, more shapes would be a good idea.

5. *What books did I use?* Mandell, Muriel, *Complete Science Course for Young Experimenters.* New York: Sterling, 1979.

1. Ballistics: Where Will It Land? (Title)

2.   *Purpose:* The purpose of this experiment is to find out how the angle of launch affects how far an object will travel. Since the experiment will be performed inside, a dart gun was chosen as the launcher. The dart gun purchased came with small, flexible darts that would not hurt anyone or anything. I wanted to see at what angle the darts will travel the farthest. My hypothesis or prediction is that the darts will travel farthest if they are shot straight ahead *(dart gun horizontal with 0-degree angle)*.

3.   *Materials:*

        Dart gun
        Tape measure
        Darts
        Washable paint
        Protractor
        Masking tape
        Plywood 2' x 2'
        Wooden meter stick

4.   *Procedure:* I used the protractor to mark various angles on the piece of wood. I drilled a hole in the end of the meter stick and used the top of the meter stick as the zero angle. I decided to try the experiment at 0, 15, 30, 45, 60, 75, and 90 degrees. I dipped the end of the dart into paint so it would mark the floor at the place where it first landed. I was careful to always hold the tip of the gun at the end of the meter stick. Also, I always held the gun right alongside the meter stick. I used a piece of masking tape to mark the location of the launch line. The tip of the meter stick in the zero position was marked as the launch line. Each time I changed the angle, I had to move the launcher forward so that I could keep the tip of the meter stick on the launch line. I measured how far the darts traveled from the launch line at each angle.

Variables:

a. What did I change? *(Manipulated variable)* The angle of the dart gun was changed.

b. What changed as a result of what I did? *(Responding variable)* The distance the darts traveled changed.

c. What things did I keep the same? *(Controls)* The gun, the darts, and the launch line were kept the same. I also made sure there were no windows or doors open so that there was no wind to affect my results.

5. *Results:*

TABLE 1	**TABLE OF MEASUREMENTS**						
	DISTANCE DART TRAVELED, FT						
TRIAL	ANGLE, DEGREES						
	0	15	30	45	60	75	90
1	7	12	18	21	15	14	0
2	9	14	20	22	16	15	-2
3	8	13	19	21.5	16	13	-1
4	7	12	20	20.5	15.5	14	0
5	7.5	13	18.5	21	16	14	-1
AVG.	8	13	19	21	16	14	-1

The darts which were shot at the 45-degree angle traveled the farthest.

6. & 7.   *Discussion and Conclusions:* According to the measurements of the experiment, the darts traveled the farthest when the gun was held at a 45-degree angle. Because I did not test angles 1 degree at a time, I am not positive that 45 degrees is exactly the best angle. Once I found that the best angle was about 45 degrees, I could have shot some more darts at 40 to 50 degrees in 1-degree increments. These measurements would more accurately define the best angle. I think that the darts shot at 0 degrees did not travel as far as those shot at 45 degrees because they did not have as much time to go forward before gravity made them fall to the ground. It seemed that the darts shot at 45 degrees were in the air the longest. Adding a time measurement would be interesting.

The study of how objects travel when launched is called ballistics. There are three branches of ballistics: interior, exterior, and terminal. This experiment is in the category of exterior ballistics. The launched object is called a projectile. The path that it travels is called the trajectory, and the distance the object travels is called the range. The path in the dart experiment resembles a curve called a parabola. It is gravity that makes the object curve toward earth. Air resists the movement of objects, and the fins on the darts help keep the nose pointing forward in the air. The size, weight, and shape of the object affect how far it travels because these things affect the air resistance. Air resistance slows the object and shortens how far it will travel.

I would like to try this experiment with objects of different size, weight, and shape using the same launcher to see how these factors affect my results.

8.   *Bibliography:* "Ballistics," *The World Book Encyclopedia,* Vol. 2, 1983, p. 38.
"Ballistics," *The Illustrated Encyclopedia of Invention,* Vol. 2, 1984, p. 140.

1. Sails: How Sail Shape Affects Distance *(Title)*

2.   *Purpose:* The purpose of this experiment is to determine how changing the shape of a tagboard sail attached to a cart changes the distance the cart will travel. I tried tagboard sails of the same area but different shapes attached to a toy cart. My hypothesis is that sail shape will affect the force of air on the sail and distance the cart will travel.

3.   *Materials:*

        Plastic Cart
        Fan
        Tagboard
        Tape Measure
        Masking Tape

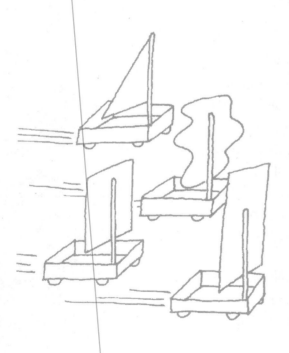

4.   *Procedure:* I cut a square out of the tagboard which was my first sail. I made another sail out of tagboard in the shape of an equilateral triangle. The third sail was a rectangle with the length 3 times as long, and the width 1/3 as long as the side of the square. Each sail had the same area as the original square. I attached the square sail to the cart and supported it with a tagboard brace. I used the same brace with each sail so I could be sure that my cart always weighed the same with each sail and there was no other geometry change besides the sail itself. I set the cart at the starting line directly in front of the fan. I turned the fan on "high" and waited for the cart to stop moving. I always recorded the distance from the starting line to the cart's front wheels. I tested each sail shape 3 times and then averaged the distances.

Variables:

a.   What did I change? *(Manipulated variable)* The shape of the sail was changed.

b.   What changed as a result of what I did? *(Responding variable)* The distance the cart traveled changed.

c.   What things did I keep the same? *(Controls)*
I kept the same area of the sail, the same fan, cart, and starting line.

5.   *Results:* The square and equilateral triangle sails traveled about the same distance while the long, thin rectangle traveled about half as far.

TABLE 1	**TABLE OF MEASUREMENTS**		
	DISTANCE CART TRAVELED, FT		
TRIAL	SHAPE OF SAIL		
	SQUARE	TRIANGLE	RECTANGLE
1	15	14	8
2	14	14	7
3	15	14.5	7.5
AVG.	15	14	8

The square and equilateral triangle sails traveled about the same distance while the long, pthin rectangle traveled about half as far.

6. & 7.   *Discussion and Conclusions:* The cart nearly went the same distance each time with the square and triangular sails, but the unusual shape of the long thin rectangle only moved the cart about half as far. It does not matter what shape the sail is as long as each sail is the same size and roughly the same shape *(like the equal-sided triangle and square).* I read about sailboats, and I think that if more shapes were tested, more differences would occur. The experiment would be better because there would be many more measurements and shapes involved. This idea would make a good experiment for another time.

I think that sometimes the distance the cart traveled was different because I did not line up the cart straight in front of the fan. Also, I think it would be a good idea to clean the floor and the wheels between each trial to make sure that no dirt is interfering with the cart. It is important to use a level floor during his experiment.

In reading about sails and sailboats, I found that there is a difference in the forces on sails if the wind comes directly from behind the sail as in the cart experiment, or if the wind meets the sail from the side. It would make an interesting experiment to retest the three sails with the wind from the side. *(The sails would have to be at some angle along the cart.)* The question would be whether the results would be about the same or if there would be more difference between the square and triangular sails.

In my reading, I noticed that when sailboats "run" before the wind like the cart in front of the fan, the sails are balloonlike in shape. In fact, they are sometimes called balloon spinnaker sails. It would make an interesting experiment to test the depth of a sail on the cart. A square cardboard sail could be made as a box with different depths and the distance traveled by the cart could be compared to the flat square sail already tested. I think I will try this experiment next year.

It would be interesting to make the sails out of cloth. Also, as I said before, more shapes would be a good idea.

8. *Bibliography:* Mandell, Muriel, *Complete Science Course for Young Experimenters.* New York: Sterling, 1979.

Notes for Kickoff Assembly Presenter

These notes are directed toward the sail shape experiment reviewed previously. However, the general ideas should be applied to all Kickoff Assembly experiments.

1. Hang a large white paper chart on the wall before the students arrive, and set up the overhead projector and chalkboard. The items to fill in the wall chart are on construction paper balloons or clouds. These items should be taped to the wall near, but not on, the chart.

2. When the students arrive, introduce yourself and tell why you are there. Then review the headings on the wall chart.

    Primary Grades:

    What is the question I want to answer?
    What do I predict will happen?
    What am I going to change?
    What happens as a result of what
        I change?
    What things do I keep the same?
    What is the answer to my question?

    Intermediate Grades:

    Question
    Hypothesis
    Manipulated Variable
    Responding Variable
    Controls
    Conclusion

    This process will give you an opportunity to review elements of the scientific method before you begin the experiment.

3. Allow students to see what you have brought to do the experiment. Point out that these are things they might have at home or can easily purchase.

4. Have a student find the question and place it in the correct box on the chart.

5. Select another student to find and place the hypothesis.

Do the same with the remaining categories until the chart is complete.

6. Select your student helpers.

7. Do one trial and don't have anyone write anything down. You will then be able to point out why the chalkboard is there and why it is necessary to record results. You can get one of the older primary students to record the data.

8. After three trials with each experiment, have the students pick a representative number from the three trials. For the intermediate grades, the student recording the data can calculate and record the averages. This result *(the average or the representative number)* will be the number to use on the bar graph on the overhead projector.

9. Graph the measurements and discuss what happened *(results)*. Have students determine the conclusion.

10. You can go over the report, time permitting. It is on an overhead. Read each section slowly and explain the contents.

11. You will have to watch your own time. The teachers will probably not interrupt you.

12. If you have time, it is a good idea to discuss the ways your experiment could have been improved, possible sources of error, and even have the students suggest modifications that might provide an interesting idea for their own science project.

Good Luck!

Appendix **E**

ADDITIONAL FORMS

The materials in this appendix are additional forms that you can copy
and adapt to your own needs. The figure numbers in parentheses
below indicate where you will find a filled-in example of a particular
form elsewhere in this book.

If you purchased the *Not Just Another Science Fair* Disk with
this book or separately, you will find these forms on the disk. You can
edit and style them as text files in WordPerfect 5.1.

1. Letter to Student Confirming Participation *(FIGURE 2.3)*
2. Science Fair Community Invitation Flier *(FIGURE 2.4)*
3. Letter to Prospective Judges *(FIGURE 4.2)*
4. Student/Parent Workshop and Science Fair
   Announcement Flier *(FIGURE 2.7)*
5. Judging Time Inquiries *(FIGURE 2.16)*

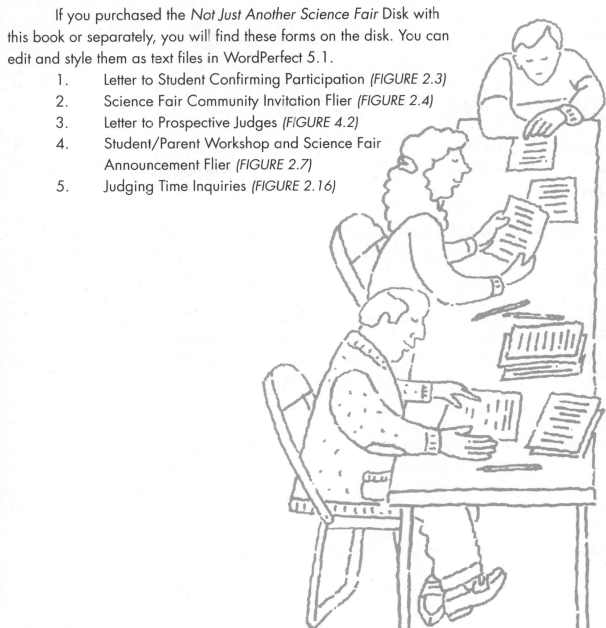

1. LETTER TO STUDENT CONFIRMING PARTICIPATION

_____, 19 ___

Dear Science Fair Participant:

This letter is to confirm your participation in the Science Fair scheduled for Saturday, _____, 19 ___. Below, we have listed several important reminders for that day:

1. Friday, _____, is set-up and check-in. Please arrive at the school with your project between _____ and _____ p.m. *NO LATE SET-UP WILL BE ALLOWED.*

2. Judging will begin at _____ a.m. Saturday. There will be special activities for participants waiting to be judged.

3. We will have phone numbers available if you wish to call Saturday morning to find out what time you will be judged. Please arrive 15 minutes prior to your scheduled judging time.

4. The fair will be open to the public from _____ to _____ p.m. on Saturday. We encourage you to stand by your projects so you can answer questions for the public.

5. You are to write your own project summary. Make sure you answer the questions that were listed in the *Science Fair Handbook*. A copy of those pages is attached. *YOUR PROJECT SUMMARY WILL BE DUE THE MONDAY BEFORE THE FAIR. PLEASE GIVE IT TO YOUR LIAISON TEACHER ON MONDAY, _____, BEFORE _____ p.m.*

    You will be given a copy of your title page as your receipt. You will *NOT* have to bring another copy of your paper to the fair.

6. The decision of the judges is final.

7. Questions about rules? Contact your school liaison teacher.

2

A
SCIENCE
FAIR
INVITATION

The entries are on the starting line!

The BIG day has finally arrived...

The _____

SCIENCE FAIR

Saturday, _____

Public Viewing _____ – _____ **p.m**

SEE THE BEST JUNIOR SCIENTISTS
GO FOR THE BLUE !

Awards Presentation

_____ – _____ **p.m.**

at _____

3. LETTER TO PROSPECTIVE JUDGES

_____, 19_____

Dear Prospective Judge:

We are writing to encourage you to join in our efforts to stimulate young minds in developing an interest in science. On Saturday, _____, 19____, _____ and _____ will be hosting its First Annual Science Fair, which involves the voluntary participation of students in grades K through 8. Thanks to the partnership of community volunteers and the school district, we hope to have successful fairs for years to come.

Because we need judges with technical *(or education)* backgrounds, we invite you to join us as one of our Science Fair judges. Judges work in teams of two composed of a technical judge and an educator; participation requires approximately _____ hours of your time on _____, from _____ to _____. Judges can preview the projects and summary reports from _____ to _____ on Friday, _____, and from _____ to _____, _____. *(Attendance at previews is optional.)*

We are emphasizing the application of the scientific method in students' projects. Students are asked to do experiments, as opposed to demonstrations or collections. The overall intent of the fair is to nurture and develop inquiring minds through the application of science.

If you wish to join in this important endeavor, please call me or complete the information below and return it to me by _____, 19____. Your assistance is appreciated.

Sincerely,

_____   _____

                                                                                   (Phone)

☐ I will serve as a judge on _____.   ☐ I cannot serve as a judge.

Name _____

Address _____

Phone _____

Best time to call _____

Grade level preference _____

THE
SCIENCE FAIR
IS
COMING

_____ , 19 _____

THIS YEAR'S THEME IS _____

A Workshop will be held at _____ School

at _____ p.m.

KINDERGARTEN–8TH-GRADE STUDENTS AND PARENTS

There will be:
- Science demonstratiions
- Teachers, parents, and scientists to help you choose a project
- Science experiments to try
- Movie on the scientific method
- Display of library books on science
- Directions for participating in the science fair
- Activities for preschool children

5. JUDGING TIME INQUIRIES

ATTENTION ALL PARENTS AND JUNIOR SCIENTISTS

As you know, Science Fair judging will begin

at .... a.m.

If you would like to know exactly what time your project is to be judged, please call one of the phone numbers listed below between _____ a.m. and _____ a.m. tomorrow morning _____, 19_____.

Please be considerate and observe the time limits. Do not call before _____ a.m. Please arrive 15–20 minutes before the assigned time.0000

Names and numbers to call:

_____

_____

_____

_____

_____

_____

_____

ALSO AVAILABLE

· ·

FROM YOUR LOCAL SCHOOL SUPPLY STORE

Not Just Another Science Fair by Laura Vazquez,
David M. France, and Kim M. Perkins 0-673-36132-2
(book only)

Not Just Another Science Fair by Laura Vazquez,
David M. France, and Kim M. Perkins 0-673-36133-0
(3.5" disk for IBM and compatible computers)

Not Just Another Science Fair by Laura Vazquez,
David M. France, and Kim M. Perkins 0-673-36134-9
(book and 3.5" disk for IBM and compatible computers)

Not Just Another Science Fair by Laura Vazquez,
David M. France, and Kim M. Perkins 0-673-36178-0
(3.5" disk for Macintosh computers)

Not Just Another Science Fair by Laura Vazquez,
David M. France, and Kim M. Perkins 0-673-36212-4
(book and 3.5" disk for Macintosh computers)

· ·